Grammar Essentials

by Geraldine Woods
with Joan Friedman

for dummies®

A Wiley Brand

Grammar Essentials For Dummies®

Published by: **John Wiley & Sons, Inc.**, 111 River Street, Hoboken, NJ 07030-5774, www.wiley.com

Copyright © 2019 by John Wiley & Sons, Inc., Hoboken, New Jersey

Published simultaneously in Canada

For general information on our other products and services, please contact our Customer Care Department within the U.S. at 877-762-2974, outside the U.S. at 317-572-3993, or fax 317-572-4002. For technical support, please visit https://hub.wiley.com/community/support/dummies.

Wiley publishes in a variety of print and electronic formats and by print-on-demand. Some material included with standard print versions of this book may not be included in e-books or in print-on-demand. If this book refers to media such as a CD or DVD that is not included in the version you purchased, you may download this material at http://booksupport.wiley.com. For more information about Wiley products, visit www.wiley.com.

Library of Congress Control Number: 2019931672

ISBN: 978-1-119-58961-7 (pbk); ISBN: 978-1-119-58967-9 (ePDF); ISBN: 978-1-119-58968-6 (ePub)

Manufactured in the United States of America

SKY10056588_092823

Contents at a Glance

Table of Contents

Introduction

When you're a grammarian, people react to you in interesting — and sometimes downright strange — ways. An elderly man once asked me about something that had puzzled him for eight decades: Why did his church, St. Paul's, include an apostrophe in its name? My nephew recently called to inquire whether his company's sign in Times Square should include a semicolon. (I said no, though the notion of a two-story-tall neon semicolon *was* tempting.) Lots of people become tongue-tied, sure that I'll judge their choice of *who* or *whom*. (They worry needlessly, because I consider myself off-duty when I'm not teaching or writing.)

Though you may aspire to be something other than a grammarian, knowing how to use proper grammar is always an advantage — especially in the workplace. Most jobs that provide you with a desk (and many jobs that don't!) demand that you know how to communicate in both speech and writing.

If you haven't yet reached the workplace, now's the best time to master good grammar. No matter what subject you're studying, teachers favor proper English. Also, the SAT includes a writing section that's heavy on grammar and, ironically, light on writing.

In this book, I show you the tricks of the grammar trade, the strategies that help you make the right decision when you're facing such grammatical dilemmas as the choice between *I* and *me* or *was* and *were*. I explain what you need to do in such situations, and I also tell you why a particular word is correct or incorrect. You don't have to memorize a list of meaningless rules (with the exception of some points from the punctuation chapter) because when you understand the reason for a particular choice, you'll pick the correct word automatically.

About This Book

I concentrate on what English teachers call the common errors. You don't have to read this book in order, and you don't have to read the whole thing. Just browse through the table of contents and look for things that you often get wrong. Or start with

Chapter 1, which outlines the usage issues voted "most likely to succeed" — in giving you a headache. When you recognize something that nags you every time you write, jump to the chapter where I explain how to handle it like a pro.

Conventions Used in This Book

When I introduce a term or concept that may be unfamiliar to you, I *italicize* it so you know I'm aware that jargon is at hand. I quickly follow it up with an explanation or definition so you can continue on with the topic.

Foolish Assumptions

I assume that you already speak English to some extent and that you want to speak it — and write it — better. I also assume that you're a busy person with better things to do than worry about pronouns. This book is for you if you want

>> Better grades

>> Skill in communicating exactly what you mean

>> A higher-paying or higher-status job

>> Speech and writing that presents you as an educated, intelligent person

>> A good score on the SAT I Writing or the ACT exam

>> Polished skills in English as a second language

Icons Used in This Book

In the left margins of this book, you find the following four icons, each of which highlights a particular type of material:

This icon points out a nugget of information you'll want to recall later, so make room for it in your mental filing cabinet.

REMEMBER

TEST ALERT Are you hoping to spend some time behind ivy-covered walls? To put it another way: Are you aiming for college? If so, you should pay special attention to the information next to this icon, because college-admissions testers *love* this material.

TIP Wherever you see this icon, you'll find helpful strategies for understanding sentence structure or choosing the correct word.

WARNING Not every grammar trick has a built-in trap, but some do. This icon tells you how to avoid common mistakes.

Where to Go from Here

Need some pointers on how to improve your writing — fast? Jump to Chapter 11. Want to refresh your memory regarding punctuation regulations? Head straight for Chapter 7. Not sure where to begin? Chapter 1 can help.

I truly don't mind where you start. Just allow me one last word before you do. Actually, two last words: *Trust yourself.* You already know a lot. If you're a native speaker, you've communicated in English all your life, including the years before you set foot in school and saw your first textbook. If English is an acquired language for you, you've probably already absorbed a fair amount of vocabulary and grammar, even if you don't know the technical terms.

I'm just here to help you refine what you know and get past any grammar gremlins that haunt you. So if the word *grammar* usually makes you sweat, wipe your brow and remember that nothing in this book is too difficult for you to master.

IN THIS CHAPTER

» Defining what *grammar* means

» Identifying the problems grammar can solve

» Bringing grammar into the real world

Chapter **1**

Grasping Grammar Nitty-Gritty

'm well aware that you've been studying grammar in one form or another for a lot of years. You may have been in first or second grade when a teacher introduced the notion that different words in a sentence do different things: Some words name people, animals, and objects, for example, and other words indicate what those people, animals, and objects are doing.

If you were blessed with brilliant, enlightened teachers, your experience with grammar has led you to understand not only how to use it but also why it's essential. However, because you're holding this book in your hands, I suspect that may not have been the case. More likely, you were blessed with caring, dedicated teachers who followed a pattern of instruction handed down to them from teachers past. That pattern likely focused on memorizing parts of speech and diagramming sentences. And here you are, years later, trying to recall what indirect objects are and why you should care.

In this chapter, I explain how I approach the study of grammar in this book. A clue: I honestly don't care whether you can identify an indirect object (a part of speech I describe in Chapter 4). I do, however, care a great deal about your ability to construct a complete sentence that communicates information clearly and meets the needs of your audience.

Grammar: What It Is!

In the Middle Ages (a few years before I went to school), *grammar* meant the study of Latin, the language of choice for educated people. In fact, grammar was so closely associated with Latin that the word referred to any kind of learning. This meaning of *grammar* shows up when people of grandparent age talk about their *grammar school*, not their elementary school. The term *grammar school* is a leftover from the old days.

These days, *grammar* is the study of language — specifically, how words are put together. Because of obsessive English teachers and their rules, *grammar* also means a set of standards that you have to follow in order to speak and write better. However, the definition of *better* changes according to your situation, your purpose, and your audience. (I discuss this subject more in the final section of this chapter, as well as in Chapter 11, where I offer tips on how to become a better writer.)

Actually, several different types of grammar exist, including *historical* (how language has changed through the centuries) and *comparative* (how languages differ from or resemble each other). In this book, I deal with only two types of grammar — the two you need to know in order to improve your speech and writing:

>> **Descriptive grammar:** This type of grammar gives names to the parts of speech and parts of a sentence. When you learn descriptive grammar, you understand what every word is (its part of speech) and what every word does (its function in the sentence).

REMEMBER

Knowing some grammar terms can help you understand why a particular word or phrase is correct or incorrect, so I sprinkle descriptive grammar terms throughout this book. However, you don't need to be able to explain the difference between a participle and a gerund to use them correctly. My main purpose is to show you how to put words together in appropriate ways so you can write a school assignment, a report for work, or any other formal communication effectively. That's why descriptive grammar plays second fiddle in this book to the type I describe in the next bullet.

» **Functional grammar:** The bulk of this book is devoted to *functional grammar,* which shows you how words behave when they're doing their jobs properly. Functional grammar guides you to the right expression — the one that fits what you're trying to say — by ensuring that the sentence is put together correctly. When you're agonizing over whether to say *I* or *me,* you're solving a problem of functional grammar.

So here's the formula for success: A little descriptive grammar plus a lot of functional grammar equals better grammar overall.

The Big Ideas of Grammar

When you get right down to it, the study of grammar is the study of three key issues: choosing the right words to get your point across to a reader or listener, putting those words in the right order, and (when you're writing) inserting the correct punctuation marks (commas, apostrophes, and so on) in the correct places. In this section, I explain why each issue matters so much.

Making the right word choices

This issue is an umbrella that covers many grammar gremlins. Four of the biggest are selecting verb forms that match the subjects in your sentence, using the right pronouns, deciding between adjectives and adverbs, and choosing wisely between two (or more) words that sound similar or seem to be interchangeable (but aren't).

Creating subject-verb harmony

Say you're writing a sentence that describes what three people are doing:

Ralph, Lulu, and Stan is skipping through the woods.

Do you detect a problem? Even if you can't put your finger on what's wrong, you probably realize that something about this sentence doesn't sound right. That "something" is the verb *is,* which doesn't get along with *Ralph, Lulu, and Stan.*

In grammatical terms, what you have here is a subject-verb disagreement. The *subject* of a sentence is the *noun* (person, place, thing, or idea) that is doing or being something. The *verb* is the part of the sentence that explains what the subject is doing.

To make the multiple (or *plural*) subjects in this sentence play nice with the verb, you must change *is* to *are*:

> Ralph, Lulu, and Stan are skipping through the woods.

Subject-verb agreement can get complicated sometimes, and I devote Chapter 2 to refreshing your memory about how to identify subjects and verbs and how to create harmony between them.

Selecting pronouns

Allow me to tell you a riveting story:

> My brother and me went to the store yesterday to look for some new dish towels. We looked in every department but couldn't find it anywhere. We asked a salesman for help, but they couldn't answer our question.

Aside from "riveting" being an out-and-out lie, can you figure out what's wrong with this story? This example contains three grammatical errors, all of which are problems with pronoun selection.

REMEMBER

A *pronoun* is a word that substitutes for a noun, and figuring out which pronoun to use in a sentence can sometimes be truly challenging. Choosing incorrectly can offend your reader's ear and also create confusion.

To correct this story, you need to make the following changes (shown in italics):

> My brother and *I* went to the store yesterday to look for some new dish towels. We looked in every department but couldn't find *them* anywhere. We asked a salesman for help, but *he* couldn't answer our question.

Not sure why you need *I* instead of *me* or *he* instead of *they*? Chapter 3 offers a detailed discussion of how to make good pronoun choices; be sure to check it out.

Describing nouns and verbs with the right words

The reason you're reading this chapter is that you want to write good, right? Actually, no. What you really want to do is to write *well*. The grammatical explanation is that *good* is always an *adjective*: a word used to describe nouns. *Well*, on the other hand, is usually an *adverb*: a word that describes a verb or modifies an adjective. But even if you never memorize the grammatical reason, you must know when to use *good* and when to use *well*.

Likewise, you need to know when to use an adjective versus when to use an adverb. Luckily, Chapter 6 provides all the details, so you'll never again feel *bad* (as opposed to *badly*) about your writing.

Choosing between similar words

If *you're* going to write well, *your* word choices have to be correct. In some cases, you choose *among* several words that sound alike. In others, you choose *between* two words that most people (incorrectly) believe to be interchangeable. *Sometimes* the choices are tricky, but if you spend *some time* reading Chapter 9, I can help.

Arranging words for optimal understanding

In this book, I commit a particular grammatical sin that wouldn't be acceptable in a more formal type of writing: I write *fragments*, which are incomplete sentences. Like this one. And this one.

The opposite of a fragment is a *run-on* sentence: one that keeps going long after it should have stopped. For example, I create a run-on if I use a comma to try to join two complete sentences, I should use a semicolon or a *conjunction* (such as *and, or,* or *but*) instead. (That was intentional, mind you. I do have my certified grammarian's license.)

Fragments and run-ons are two problems writers grapple with when trying to create complete sentences. Other problems can be a bit tougher to identify, such as combining ideas of unequal importance in ways that make them seem equal. Consider an example:

First idea: I tripped and broke my leg.

Second idea: I was chewing gum.

Combination: I tripped and broke my leg, and I was chewing gum.

Technically, the combined sentence is okay. But are you really helping the reader understand what happened here? Just by changing *and* to a different connecting word, you can clarify what happened. For example:

I tripped and broke my leg *while* I was chewing gum.

I tripped and broke my leg *because* I was chewing gum.

I devote Chapter 4 to a thorough discussion of how to create complete sentences that provide the reader with an appropriate amount of information arranged in a helpful way.

Chapter 5 tackles still more issues related to word arrangement, such as making sentences parallel. Take a look at a sentence that isn't parallel:

My goal is to study economics, Arabic, and impress my boss.

What you're saying is that you plan to study three things, the third being "impress my boss." Huh? By making the sentence parallel, you clarify for your reader what you actually mean:

My goal is to study economics, *learn* Arabic, and impress my boss.

By adding *learn*, you start each of the three items in your list with a verb, which makes the sentence parallel.

Chapter 5 deals with several other word arrangement issues as well, with the goal of helping you create clear, consistent writing.

Pinpointing punctuation

Its a real shame, when you write a perfectly fine sentence; and mess it up with 'improper' punctuation.

REMEMBER

We all need occasional reminders about how to use punctuation marks. So many rules exist, and not all of them make logical sense. Your job is not to argue the logic; it's to apply the rules to every sentence you write. If you don't, your boss, teacher, or other authority figure is likely to dismiss your written observations because he or she won't be able to look past the errors to discover your brilliance.

To impress someone with your writing, you simply must know the punctuation rules and use punctuation marks correctly. That's why I suggest getting very cozy with Chapter 7. After all,

> It's a real shame when you write a perfectly fine sentence and mess it up with improper punctuation.

Oh, and if you ever get confused about when to use capital letters and when to stick with lowercase, be sure to check out Chapter 8.

Putting Grammar to Work in the Real World

The grammar lessons in this book are useless if they don't stick with you when you sit down to write. I strongly suggest keeping this book handy as a reference whenever you're working on an assignment or report; I don't expect you to memorize every punctuation or capitalization rule.

However, I work hard to bring the lessons in this book to life for you by providing lots of examples. The goal is for your "ear" — the part of your brain that can tell whether something you've written sounds right or wrong — to get lots of practice identifying common problems.

You can improve your grammar ear in lots of easy ways every day. Chapter 12 offers ten simple suggestions that range from reading good books, newspapers, and magazines to listening to news radio programs and watching quality TV shows in which the characters use proper English. (Think the History Channel, for example — not so much *The Sopranos*.)

The more you read and listen, the easier you'll be able to identify situations in which formal (or *standard*) English is required and situations in which you can relax the rules a bit. In Chapter 11, I explain the differences between formal and conversational English and note that just about any important communication requires formal English.

WARNING

You may have the impression, for example, that you can relax the grammar rules when you're writing an e-mail or a text message. But as I explain in Chapter 11, the medium conveying your message isn't the deciding factor; your *audience* is. Who is going to read your e-mail or text message? Your best friend? Break as many grammar rules as you want. Your boss or teacher? Keep it formal. Even if you suspect that the individual won't mind a conversational tone, you don't want to risk a miscommunication, and you don't want a grammatically lax e-mail to be forwarded. Save yourself any potential embarrassment or hassle: Keep it formal.

Chapter 11 offers lots of other suggestions for improving your writing as well, including choosing juicy verbs and eliminating repetition. But in the end, the only way to improve your writing is to write. Reading a book — even one as astute and inspiring as this one — can take you only so far. Practice is essential, so dedicate a small amount of time every day to improving your speech and writing. Before long, you may start noticing billboards, store signs, and even newspaper headlines with grammatical errors. At that point, you'll be ready to apply for your official grammarian's license, too. (Calm down, now. Your heart may not be able to handle this much excitement.)

Chapter **2**
Making Peace between Subjects and Verbs

I n every sentence, you find two key pieces of information: an action or a state of being, and the someone or something that is doing that action or experiencing that state of being. The acting or being part is expressed by a *verb*. The someone or something part is represented by a *subject*.

You probably have lots of experience finding subjects and verbs; that task begins in early elementary school and doesn't let up until you're holding a diploma. That's why I don't go into great depth explaining what subjects and verbs are in this chapter; I just offer some rapid reminders.

I then move on to making subjects and verbs agree with each other. That task is a bit more difficult, and the presence of certain subjects and verbs makes it even more challenging. I cover the trickiest types of subject/verb pairings here because I assume they're likely the reason you're cozying up with this chapter.

If your subjects and verbs have disagreed in the past, fear not: This chapter can help you get them working in harmony.

Getting Reacquainted with Verbs

All sentences contain verbs — words that express action or a state of being. Verbs come in all shapes and sizes. In this section, I remind you how to distinguish between linking and action verbs and how to sort helping verbs from main verbs. I also touch on compound verbs and some tricky verb imposters: infinitives.

Linking verbs: The giant equal sign

Linking verbs are also called *being verbs* because they express states of being: what is, will be, or was. Here's where math intersects with English: Linking verbs are like giant equal signs plopped into the middle of your sentence. For example, you can think of the sentence

Ralph's uncle *is* a cannibal with a taste for finger food.

as

Ralph's uncle = a cannibal with a taste for finger food.

Or, in shortened form,

Ralph's uncle = a cannibal.

The word *is* links two ideas and says that they're the same. Thus, *is* is a linking verb. Here are more linking verbs:

Lulu *will be* angry when she hears about the missing bronze tooth. (Lulu = angry; *will be* is a linking verb.)

Stan *was* the last surfer to leave the water when the tidal wave approached. (Stan = the last surfer; *was* is a linking verb.)

Edgar *has been* depressed ever since the fall of the House of Usher. (Edgar = depressed; *has been* is a linking verb.)

You may have noticed that all the linking verbs in the sample sentences are forms of the verb *to be*. That's not always the case, though. Check out these examples of other linking verbs:

With his foot-long fingernails and sly smile, Big Foot *seemed* threatening. (Big Foot = threatening; *seemed* is a linking verb.)

A jail sentence for the unauthorized use of a comma *appears* harsh. (jail sentence = harsh; *appears* is a linking verb in this sentence.)

The penalty for making a grammar error *remains* severe. (penalty = severe; *remains* is a linking verb in this sentence.)

Loch Ness *stays* silent whenever monsters are mentioned. (Loch Ness = silent; *stays* is a linking verb in this sentence.)

Seemed, appears, remains, and *stays* are similar to forms of the verb *to be* in that they express states of being. They simply add shades of meaning to the basic concept.

TIP

Sensory verbs — verbs that express information you receive through sight, hearing, smell, taste, and touch — may also be linking verbs:

Two minutes after shaving, Ralph's double chin *feels* scratchy. (Ralph's double chin = scratchy; *feels* is a linking verb.)

The 10-year-old lasagna in your refrigerator *smells* disgusting. (lasagna = disgusting; *smells* is a linking verb.)

WARNING

Verbs that refer to the five senses are linking verbs only if they act as an equal sign in the sentence. If they don't equate two ideas, they aren't linking verbs. In the preceding example sentence about Ralph's double chin, *feels* is a linking verb. Here's a different sentence with the same verb:

With her delicate fingers, Lulu *feels* Ralph's chin.

In this sentence, *feels* is not a linking verb because you're not saying that

Lulu = chin.

Instead, you're saying that Lulu doesn't believe that Ralph shaved, so she goes stubble hunting. In this case, *feels* is an action verb (which I explain next).

REMEMBER

Bottom line: Any verb that figuratively places an equal sign in the sentence is a linking verb.

Action verbs: The go-getters

Linking verbs are important, but unless you're in some sort of hippie commune left over from the '60s, you just can't sit around *being* all the time. You have to do something. Here's where action verbs come into the picture. Everything that is not *being* is *action*, at least in the verb world. Unlike the giant equal sign associated with linking verbs, something *happens* with an action verb:

> Drew *slapped* the offending pig right on the snout. (*Slapped* is an action verb.)

> Fred *will steal* third base as soon as his sneezing fit *ends*. (*Will steal* and *ends* are action verbs.)

> According to the teacher, Roger *has shot* at least 16 spitballs in the last ten minutes. (*Has shot* is an action verb.)

WARNING

Don't let the name *action* fool you. Some action verbs aren't particularly energetic: *think, sit, stay, have, sleep,* and *dream* are examples. Think of the definition this way: If the verb is not a giant equal sign (a linking verb), it's an action verb.

Helping verbs: The do-gooders

Some of the verbs I identify in this chapter are single words, and others are made up of two or more words. The extra words are called *helping verbs*. They don't take out the trash or dust the living room, but they do help the main verb express meaning, usually by changing the time, or *tense*, of the action.

Here are some sentences with helping verbs:

> Alice *will have sung* five arias from that opera by the time her recorder *runs* out of tape. (In *will have sung, sung* is the main verb; *will* and *have* are helping verbs. Later in the sentence, *runs* is a main verb without a helping verb.)

> Larry *should have refused* to play the part of the villain, but his ego simply *would* not *be denied*. (In *should have refused, refused* is the main verb; *should* and *have* are helping verbs. In *would be denied, denied* is the main verb; *would* and *be* are helping verbs.)

Distinguishing between helping verbs and main verbs isn't particularly important, as long as you get the whole thing when you're identifying the verb in a sentence. If you find only part of the verb, you may confuse action verbs with linking verbs.

TIP

To decide whether you have an action verb or a linking verb, look at the main verb, not at the helping verbs. If the main verb expresses action, the whole verb is action, even if one of the helpers is a form of *to be*. For example,

> is going

> has been painted

> should be strangled

are all action verbs, not linking verbs, because *going, painted,* and *strangled* express action.

Doubling your money: Compound verbs

You can pair a single subject in a sentence with two (or more) verbs. For example:

> Justin's ex-girlfriend *burped* and *cried* after the contest.

You have two actions *(burped, cried)* and one person doing both *(ex-girlfriend).*

In grammatical terms, these double verbs are called *compound verbs.* Here are two more examples:

> George *snatched* the atomic secret and quickly *stashed* it in his navel. *(snatched, stashed* = verbs)

> Ella *ranted* for hours about Larry's refusal to hold an engagement party and then *crept* home. *(ranted, crept* = verbs)

Infinitives: Verb imposters

You may hear English teachers say "the verb *to sweep*" or some such expression. In fact, in this chapter I refer to "the verb *to be.*" But *to be* is not actually a verb; it's an infinitive. An *infinitive* is *to + a verb.* Other examples of infinitives include *to laugh, to sing, to burp, to write,* and *to think.*

The most important thing to know about infinitives is this: When you need to find the verb of a sentence, don't choose an infinitive as your answer. If you do, you'll miss the real verb or verbs in the sentence. Other than that, forget about infinitives!

Okay, you can't forget about infinitives completely. Here's something else you should know about infinitives in formal English: Don't split them in half. For example, you commonly see sentences like the following:

> Matt vowed to really study if he ever got the chance to take the flight instructor exam again.

This example is common, but incorrect. Grammatically, *to study* is a unit — one infinitive. You're not supposed to separate its two halves. Now that you know this rule, read the newspaper. Everybody splits infinitives, even the grayest, dullest papers with no comics whatsoever. So you have two choices: You can split infinitives all you want, or you can follow the rule and feel totally superior to the professional journalists. The choice is yours.

Identifying Subjects

All sentences contain verbs — words that express action or a state of being. But you can't have an action in a vacuum. You can't have a naked, solitary state of being, either. Someone or something must also be present in the sentence — the *who* or *what* that you're talking about in relation to the action or state of being that the verb expresses. This someone or something doing the action or experiencing the state of being is the *subject*.

A someone is a person, of course, and a something must be a thing, place, or idea. That means the subject is usually a noun, because a noun is a person, place, thing, or idea. I say *usually* because sometimes the subject is a *pronoun* — a word that substitutes for a noun (such as *he, they,* or *it*). For details on pronouns, check out Chapter 3.

Subjects aren't always as straightforward as they seem. In the following sections, I explain some of the finer points of subjects, including how to find the subject when it appears to be missing or in hiding.

Getting two for the price of one: Compound subjects

Earlier in the chapter I explain that you can have *compound verbs* — two or more verbs in a sentence that connect with a single subject. Well, guess what? You can also have two or more subjects that connect with one verb. The multiple subjects are called *compound subjects*. Here's an example:

> *Dorothy* and *Justin* went home in defeat.

The sentence features one action (*went*) and two people (*Dorothy, Justin*) doing the action. You have two subjects.

Here are two more examples:

> *Lola* and *Lulu* ganged up on George yesterday. (*Lola, Lulu* = subjects)

> The *omelet* and *fries* revolted Stella. (*omelet, fries* = subjects)

Figuring out you-understood

"Cross on the green, not in between."

"Eat your vegetables."

"Don't leave your chewing gum on the bedpost overnight."

What do these sentences have in common? Yes, they're all nagging comments you've heard all your life. More to the point, they're all commands. The verbs give orders: *cross, eat, don't leave.* So where's the subject in these sentences?

If you know that the verbs are *cross, eat,* and *don't leave,* your next step is to figure out who is doing the crossing, eating, and not leaving. Who is it? Uh . . .

This question appears to have no answer, but appearances can be deceiving. The answer is *you. You* cross on the green. *You* eat your vegetables. *You* don't leave your chewing gum on the bedpost overnight. What's that you say? *You* is not in the sentence? True. *You* is not written, but it's implied. And when your mom says, "Eat your vegetables," you understand that she means *you.*

Grammarians say that the subject in this type of sentence is *you-understood*. The subject is *you*, even though *you* isn't in the sentence (and even though *you* don't intend to eat any lima beans).

Finding subjects when words are missing

In the never-ending human quest to save time, words are often chopped out of sentences. The assumption is that the sentence is still understandable because the listener or reader supplies the missing piece. (Not a bad assumption, as long as you understand what you can chop and what you need to leave alone.) Check out these examples:

> If caught, Roger will probably deny everything.
>
> Lulu snored when dreaming of little sheep.

Do you understand what these sentences mean? Here they are again, with the missing words inserted and italicized:

> If *he is* caught, Roger will probably deny everything.
>
> Lulu snored when *she was* dreaming of little sheep.

In both cases, the subject and part of the verb are missing in the subordinate clauses of these sentences. (In Chapter 4, I explain that *subordinate clauses* can't stand on their own as complete sentences. "If he is caught" and "when she was dreaming of little sheep" are the subordinate clauses in these examples.) In cases like this, the reader fills in the missing information.

TIP

You need to remember only one rule for these sentences: The missing subject must be the same as the subject that is present. In other words, if your sentence lacks more information, the reader or listener will assume that you're talking about the same person or thing in both parts of the sentence. Here's an example:

> **Wrong:** If caught, his mother assumes that Roger will deny everything.
>
> **Unintended meaning:** Roger's mother is the evildoer.

A sentence like this may be most easily corrected by stating the subject in both parts of the sentence:

Correction: If Roger is caught, his mother assumes that he'll deny everything.

Grappling with unusual word order

Most of the sentences you encounter are in the normal subject-verb order, which is (gasp) subject–verb. In other words, the subject usually comes before the verb. However, not every sentence follows that order. Sometimes a subject hides out at the end of the sentence or in some other weird place. (Hey, even a subject needs a change of scenery sometimes.)

REMEMBER

No matter where the subject is hiding, you can find it by asking yourself the same question that always applies: Who or what is doing the action (or experiencing the state of being) in the sentence?

Try this example:

Up the avenue and around the park trudged Godzilla on his way to tea with the Loch Ness Monster.

What's the verb in the sentence? *Trudged* — it's the action. Who or what *trudged? Godzilla* did, so *Godzilla* is the subject. (I'll let you decide whether Godzilla is a who or a what.)

If you were answering by word order, you'd say *park*. But the *park* did not *trudge; Godzilla trudged.* Pay attention to meaning, not to placement in the sentence, and you can't go wrong.

Searching for the subject in questions

Does everyone love grammar? Don't answer that! I started this section with that sentence not to check your attitude toward grammar (I'd rather not know) but to illustrate the subject's favorite location in a question. You form most questions in English by adding a helping verb — *do, does, will, can, should,* and so forth — to a main verb. The subject is generally tucked between the helping verb and the main verb, but you don't have to bother remembering that fascinating bit of trivia.

To locate the subject in a question, simply ask the same question you'd ask with any other sentence: Who or what is doing the action (or experiencing the state of being)? In the example of "Does everyone love grammar?" the verb is *does love*. Who is doing that action? The answer is *everyone* — that's your subject.

TIP

When you're identifying the subject of a question, the questions you ask yourself may sound a little odd. Why? Because in a question, the subject usually isn't located in front of the verb. But if you ignore the awkwardness of the phrasing and concentrate on meaning, you can easily — and correctly — identify the subject of a question.

Tossing fake subjects aside

Someone comes up to you and says, "Here is one million dollars." What's the first question that comes into your mind? I know, good grammarian that you are, that your question is, "What's the subject of that sentence?" Well, try to answer your question in the usual way, by first identifying the verb. What's the action or state of being in this sentence? The answer: *is*. Okay, so who or what *is*?

What did you say? *Here is*? Wrong. *Here* can't be a subject. Neither can *there*. Both of these words are fake subjects. (*Here* and *there* are adverbs, not nouns. See Chapter 6 for more on adverbs.) What's the real answer to the question "What is"? *One million dollars. Here* and *there* are fill-ins, or place markers; they aren't what you're talking about. *One million dollars* — that's what you're talking about!

Give Peace a Chance: Making Subjects and Verbs Agree

Hollywood filmmakers and about a million songwriters have tried to convince people that opposites attract. Grammarians have clearly not gotten that message! The English language prefers matching pairs: singular with singular and plural with plural. Matching, in grammar terminology, is called *agreement*.

In this section, I show you how to make subjects and verbs agree. I first offer some easy examples of matching singular subjects with singular verbs and plural subjects with plural verbs. I then show you what happens when you're dealing with verbs that aren't exactly straightforward. And finally, I highlight some special cases — treacherous nouns and pronouns that are often mismatched.

TEST ALERT

By the way, subject-verb agreement travels so often to the SAT Writing and ACT English tests that it should earn frequent flyer miles. Test-takers, take note!

No mixing allowed: Singles and plurals

You must always pair singular subjects with singular verbs and plural subjects with plural verbs. Check out these examples:

> The ugly duckling hates the mirrored room. (*duckling* = singular subject; *hates* = singular verb)
>
> The plastic elf is still sitting on the store shelf. (*elf* = singular subject; *is sitting* = singular verb)
>
> Hedge clippers are always a thoughtful gift. (*clippers* = plural subject; *are* = plural verb)
>
> We plan to redecorate next summer. (*we* = plural subject; *plan* = plural verb)

TIP

How do you know whether a subject-verb pair should be singular or plural? Focus on the subject first. Determine the number of subjects performing the action of the sentence. If the subject is singular, the verb must be singular; if the subject is plural, the verb must be plural. You then find a verb that matches — a task that, as I explain next, isn't always simple.

Verbs that change and verbs that don't

If you're a native speaker of English, your ear helps you correctly match singular and plural subjects to their verbs most of the time. But even if English isn't your first language, you probably pair up lots of subjects and verbs correctly. That's because most verb tenses use the same form for both singular and plural verbs.

Note that I don't delve into an explanation of verb tenses here; frankly, you don't need to know how to label a verb tense in order to use it. I refer to the labels in case doing so helps jog a distant memory, but if it doesn't, just focus on the examples.

Following are some examples of the verb *to snore* in various tenses that use the same form for both singular and plural subjects:

> Larry *snored* constantly, but his cousins *snored* only occasionally.

> Ella *will snore* if she eats cheese before bedtime, but her bridesmaids *will snore* only after a meal containing sardines.

> Cedric *had snored* long before his tonsils were removed. His pet tigers *had snored* nightly before Cedric upgraded their diet.

> By the time this chapter is over, Lola *will have snored* for at least an hour, and her friends *will have snored* for an even longer period.

Unfortunately, not all verbs (in all tenses) stay the same when you shift from a singular subject to a plural subject. (If that were the case, we grammarians wouldn't be such a hot commodity.)

TIP

With regular verbs in the present tense, the difference between the singular and plural forms is often just one letter. The singular verb ends in *s* and the plural form doesn't. Here are some examples:

Singular	Plural
the tiger *bites*	the tigers *bite*
Lulu *rides*	they *ride*
she *screams*	the boys *scream*
Loch Ness *burps*	both *burp*

WARNING

Verbs that end in *-ing* (called *progressive tense*, in case you're curious) can cause singular/plural problems. They rely on the verb *to be*, a grammatical weirdo that changes drastically depending on its subject. Just be sure to match the subject of the sentence to the correct form of the verb *to be*. Check out these examples of *-ing* forms of the verb *to bite*:

>> **Singular present:** I *am biting,* you *are biting,* Dracula *is biting,* no one *is biting.*

>> **Plural present:** We *are biting,* you *are biting,* the tigers *are biting,* they *are biting.*

>> **Singular past:** I *was biting,* you *were biting,* Dracula *was biting,* no one *was biting.*

>> **Plural past:** We *were biting,* you *were biting,* the tigers *were biting,* both *were biting.*

Some lovely verb tenses called the *present perfect* and the *future perfect* contain forms of the verb *to have.* Match the subject of the sentence to the correct form of *to have,* and you'll be good to go:

>> **Present perfect:** I *have bitten,* I *have been biting,* you *have bitten,* you *have been biting,* Dracula *has bitten,* Lola *has been biting,* we *have bitten,* we *have been biting,* the tigers *have bitten,* the tigers *have been biting.*

>> **Future perfect:** I *will have bitten,* I *will have been biting,* you *will have bitten,* you *will have been biting,* Dracula *will have bitten,* Lola *will have been biting,* we *will have bitten,* we *will have been biting,* the tigers *will have bitten,* the tigers *will have been biting.*

REMEMBER

As the examples in this section demonstrate, the word *you* is both singular and plural. I can say, "You are crazy" to my neighbor when he claims that bacon is low in fat. I can also say, "You are crazy" to all those people who think Martians constructed the pyramids. In either case, I use the plural form of the verb *(are).* The fact that *you* is both singular and plural may be responsible for the popularity of such terms as *you all, y'all, youse* (very big in New York City), *you guys* (ditto), and *you people.* These terms are colorful but not correct in formal English. Because you use *you* for both singular and plural subjects, you make the meaning clear with context clues:

> Today you must all wear clothes to the Introduction to Nudism class because the heat is broken.

> "I must have you and only you!" cried Larry to his soon-to-be sixth wife.

Dealing with negative statements

You form some present-tense negative statements by adding *do* or *does,* along with the word *not,* to a main verb. The *not* squeezes itself between the helper *(do* or *does)* and the main verb. Remember that *does* is always singular. The helping verb *do* may be paired with the singular subjects *I* and *you,* and it's also used with all plural subjects. Here are some examples:

> *Larry does* not *drive* a sports car, because he wants to project a wholesome image.
>
> The killer *bees do* not *chase* Roger, because they are afraid of him.
>
> *I do* not *want* to learn anything else about verbs ever again.
>
> *You do* not *dance* like that in this club!

To form past-tense negative statements, the helping verb *did* is all you need for both singular and plural subjects:

> *Roger did* not *dance* all night.
>
> *Lola* and *Lulu did* not *send* a package of killer bees to Roger.

Negative statements in the future tense are easy as well. The helping verbs *shall* and *will* are the same for both singular and plural:

> *Roger will* not *write* a thank-you note to Lola.
>
> The killer *bees will* not *shy* away from Larry.

Cutting through distractions

Subjects and their verbs are like parents and babies on a stroll through the park; they always travel together. A passerby cooing at a baby may catch the kid's attention, but ultimately, the passerby is a distraction — irrelevant to the essential parent-child bond. The sentence world has lots of passersby that show up, slip between a subject and its verb, and distract you.

TIP

When you're trying to make your subjects and verbs agree, the best strategy is to identify distractions and then cross them out (at least mentally) to get to the bare bones of the sentence: the subject-verb pair.

REMEMBER

The most common distractions, but not the only ones, are prepositional phrases. A *prepositional phrase* contains a preposition (*on, to, for, by,* and so on) and an object of the preposition (a noun or pronoun). These phrases may contain some descriptive words as well. Other distractions may be clauses or participles. (For more information on prepositional phrases, see Chapter 10. I cover clauses and participles in Chapter 4.)

In the following sentences, I added some camouflage. The distractions (not all prepositional phrases) are italicized.

> The accountant *with 10,000 clients and only two assistants* works way too hard. (*accountant* = subject; *works* = verb)

In this sentence, *accountant* is the singular subject. If you pay attention to the prepositional phrase, you may incorrectly focus on *clients* and *assistants* as the subject — both plural words.

> The FBI agent, *fascinated by my last three tax returns,* is ruining my vacation plans. (*agent* = subject; *is ruining* = verb)

By ignoring the distracting phrase about my tax returns in this sentence, you can easily pick out the singular subject–verb pair.

> The deductions, *not the tax rate,* are a problem. (*deductions* = subject; *are* = verb)

In this sentence, *deductions* is the plural subject. If you let yourself be distracted, you may incorrectly match your verb to *rate,* which is singular.

REMEMBER

Ignore all distracting phrases and find the true subject–verb pair. Also, if any IRS employees are reading this book, please ignore my tax returns.

Coming to an Agreement with Difficult Subjects

Every family has at least one "difficult" relative — the one nobody wants to sit with on Thanksgiving. In this respect, English grammar resembles a family. Sadly, you can't dump your crazy relatives, nor can you ignore the difficult subject–verb scenarios I describe here.

Spotting five little pronouns that break the rules

In the preceding section I told you to ignore prepositional phrases when trying to make your subjects and verbs agree. Now I must confess that this rule has one small exception — well, five small exceptions. Five pronouns — five little words that just have to stir up trouble — change from singular to plural according to the prepositional phrases that follow them. The five troublemaking pronouns are

>> All

>> Any

>> Most

>> None

>> Some

TIP

A good way to remember these five important words is with this nonsense sentence:

Alice's aunt makes nice salads. (*Alice's* = all, *aunt* = any, *makes* = most, *nice* = none, *salads* = some)

Here are these pronouns with some prepositional phrases and verbs. Notice how the prepositional phrase affects the verb number.

Singular	Plural
all the pie is	*all* the shoes are
any of the information is	*any* of the magazines are
most of the city is	*most* of the pencils are
none of the pollution is	*none* of the toenails are
some of the speech is	*some* of the politicians are

REMEMBER

See the pattern? For these five words, the prepositional phrase is the determining factor. If the phrase refers to a plural idea, the verb is plural. If the phrase refers to a singular idea, the verb is singular.

Finding problems here and there

As I note earlier in the chapter, sentences that begin with *here* or *there* can trip up your efforts to work with subjects and verbs. (See the section "Tossing fake subjects aside.") In the following examples, the subject–verb pairs are italicized:

> *Here is* the *baby parakeet* that just bumped his head on the window.

> *There are* no flying *schools* for birds.

REMEMBER

As you see, the words *here* and *there* aren't italicized. These words are never subjects! The true subject in this type of sentence comes after the verb, so that's where you look when you're making a subject–verb match.

Meeting the ones, the things, and the bodies

The *Ones*, the *Things*, and the *Bodies* are families of pronouns that delight in mischief-making. They can be deceptive when you're trying to match them with verbs. (Pairing them with other pronouns can cause some trouble too; I address that topic in Chapter 3.) Take a peek at the family tree:

> The Ones: *one, everyone, someone, anyone, no one*

> The Things: *everything, something, anything, nothing*

> The Bodies: *everybody, somebody, anybody, nobody*

These pronouns are always singular, even if they're surrounded by prepositional phrases that express plurals. You must match these pronouns with singular verbs. Take a look at these examples:

> So *everybody is* happy because *no one has caused* any trouble, and *anything goes*.

> *Anyone* in the pool of candidates for dogcatcher *speaks* better than Lulu.

> *One* of the million reasons to hate you *is* your tendency to split infinitives.

> Not *one* out of a million spies *creates* as much distraction as George.

Two other pronouns are also a pain when the issue is subject/verb agreement. *Each* and *every* are very powerful words; they're strong enough to change any subject following them into a singular idea. Consider these examples:

> *Each* shoe and sock *is* in need of mending, but Larry refuses to pick up a needle and thread.
>
> *Every* dress and skirt in that store *is* on sale, and Lulu is in a spending mood.

Do these sentences look wrong to you? Granted, they appear to have plural subjects: two things *(shoe and sock)* in sentence one, and another two things *(dress and skirt)* in sentence two. But when *each* or *every* is placed in front of a group, you take the items in the group one at a time. In the first sample sentence, the subject consists of one *shoe*, one *sock*, another *shoe*, another *sock*, and so on. Therefore, the sentence needs a singular verb to match the singular subject. Ditto for the *dress and skirt* reference in the second example.

Figuring out either and neither

Two more pain-in-the-pick-your-body-part pronouns are *either* and *neither* when they're without their partners *or* and *nor*. When they're alone, *either* and *neither* are always singular, even if you insert a huge group (or just a group of two) between them and their verbs. Hence,

> *Either* of the two armies *is* strong enough to take over the entire planet.
>
> *Neither* of the football captains *has shown* any willingness to accept Lola as quarterback.

Because the sample sentences are about armies and captains, you may be tempted to choose plural verbs. Resist the temptation! No matter what the sentence says, if the subject is *either* or *neither*, singular is the correct way to go.

However, when *either* and *neither* appear with their best buds, *or* and *nor*, two things happen. First, *either* and *neither* turn into *conjunctions* (joining words). Second, if they're joining two subjects, the subject that's closer to the verb determines whether the verb is singular or plural. Yes, that's right! This is a grammar problem you can solve with a ruler. Check out these examples:

> Either *Ella* or *her bridesmaids have eaten* the icing on the cake. (*bridesmaids* = closest subject, a plural; *have eaten* = plural verb)

> Neither *the waiters* nor *Larry is planning* to eat the leftovers. (*Larry* = closest subject, a singular; *is planning* = singular verb)

Most sentences that are questions have helping verbs, and the helpers are the part of the verb that changes. Never fear: This is still grammar by ruler. The subject closest to the part of the verb that changes governs the singular/plural decision. Take a look at these examples:

> *Does* either *Ella* or *her cousins want* antacids? (*Ella* = subject closest to the helping verb *does; Ella* = singular subject; *does want* = singular verb)

> *Do* neither *her cousins* nor *Ella know* how to cook? (*cousins* = subject closest to the helping verb *do; cousins* = plural subject; *do know* = plural verb)

IN THIS CHAPTER

» **Matching pronouns with nouns**

» **Distinguishing between singular and plural pronouns**

» **Wielding possessive pronouns like a pro**

» **Selecting nonsexist pronouns**

Chapter **3**

Perfecting Your Pronoun Usage

P ronouns are words that substitute for nouns. Even though they're useful, pronouns can also be pesky because English has many different types of pronouns, each governed by its own set of rules. In this chapter I concentrate on how to avoid the most common errors associated with this part of speech.

Playing Matchmaker with Pronouns and Nouns

To make the right pronoun choices, first take a close look at how pronouns are paired with nouns. A pronoun's meaning can vary from sentence to sentence. Think of pronouns as the ultimate substitute teachers: One day they're solving quadratic equations, and the next they're doing push-ups in the gym. Such versatility comes from the fact that pronouns don't have identities of their own; instead, they stand in for nouns. In a few situations, pronouns even stand in for other pronouns. I discuss pronoun-pronoun pairs later in this chapter.

To choose the appropriate pronoun, you must consider the word that the pronoun is replacing, which is called the pronoun's *antecedent.*

Identifying the pronoun-antecedent pair is really a matter of reading comprehension. If the sentence (or in some cases, the paragraph) doesn't make the pronoun-antecedent connection clear, the writing is faulty. Time to edit! But in most cases the meaning of the pronoun leaps off the page. Take a look at some examples:

> Hal stated *his* goals clearly: *He* wanted to take over the world. (The pronouns *his* and *he* refer to the noun *Hal.*)

> The lion with a thorn in *her* paw decided to wear sneakers the next time *she* went for a walk in the jungle. (The pronouns *her* and *she* refer to the noun *lion.*)

> *Our* cause is just! Down with sugarless gum! *We* demand that all bubble gum be loaded with sugar! (The pronouns *our* and *we* refer to the speakers, who aren't named.)

> Larry, *who* types five or six words a minute, is writing a new encyclopedia. (The pronoun *who* refers to the noun *Larry.*)

> Ameba and *I* demand that the microscope be cleaned before *we* begin the exam. (The pronoun *I* refers to the speaker. The pronoun *we* refers to *Ameba and I.*)

TIP

When analyzing a sentence, you seldom find a noun that's been replaced by the pronouns *I* and *we*. The pronoun *I* always refers to the speaker, and *we* refers to the speaker and someone else.

Similarly, the pronoun *it* sometimes has no antecedent:

> *It* is raining.

> *It* is obvious that Sylvia has not won the card-flipping contest.

In these sentences, *it* is just a place-filler.

REMEMBER

Sometimes the meaning of the pronoun is explained in a previous sentence:

> Ted's ice cream *cone* is cracked. I don't want *it*. (The pronoun *it* refers to the noun *cone.*)

Selecting Singular or Plural Pronouns

All pronouns are either singular or plural. Singular pronouns replace singular nouns, which are those that name one person, place, thing, or idea. Plural pronouns replace plural nouns — those that name more than one person, place, thing, or idea. (Grammar terminology has flair, doesn't it?) A few pronouns replace other pronouns; in those situations, singular pronouns replace other singular pronouns, and plurals replace plurals. You need to understand pronoun number — singulars and plurals — before you place them in sentences. Look at Table 3-1 for a list of the singular and plural pronouns you'll encounter most often.

TABLE 3-1 Common Singular and Plural Pronouns

Singular	Plural
I	we
me	us
myself	ourselves
you	you
yourself	yourselves
he/she/it	they/them
himself/herself/itself	themselves
who	who
which	which
that	that

TIP

Notice that some of the pronouns in Table 3-1 do double duty; they take the place of both singular and plural nouns or pronouns. Lest you think this double duty makes your life easier, flip to Chapter 2 for the ins and outs of matching singular and plural subjects with their verbs.

Letting your ear be your guide

Most of the time, choosing between singular and plural pronouns is easy. You're not likely to say

> Gordon tried to pick up the ski poles, but it was too heavy.

That's because *ski poles* (plural) and *it* (singular) don't match. Instead, you say

> Gordon tried to pick up the ski poles, but they were too heavy.

Matching *ski poles* with *they* should please your ear.

TIP

If you're learning English as a second language, your ear for the language is still in training. Put it on an exercise regimen of at least an hour a day of careful listening. A radio station or a TV show in which reasonably educated people are speaking will help you to train your ear (see Chapter 12 for ideas). You'll soon become comfortable hearing and choosing the proper pronouns.

Treating companies as singular nouns

WARNING

Company and business names sometimes sound plural — for example, Saks, Lord and Taylor, and AT&T. However, a company is just one company and is, therefore, a singular noun. When you refer to the company, use the singular pronoun *it* or *its*, not the plural pronouns *they* or *their*. Take a look at these sentences, in which the singular pronouns are italicized:

> Dombey and Sons often sends *its* employees on business trips.

> *It* is offering a free vacation in the Caribbean to all *its* clerks.

TIP

If a singular pronoun sounds strange, you may adjust the sentence to refer to the employees. Sometimes you cut the pronoun entirely. Here's an example:

> **Strange:** I returned the sweater to Sheldon & Daughters Department Store, and it offered me a refund.

> **Better-sounding but wrong:** I returned the sweater to Sheldon & Daughters Department Store, and they offered me a refund.

Better-sounding and right: I returned the sweater to Sheldon & Daughters Department Store, and the sales representative offered me a refund.

Steering clear of "person" problems

Two nouns — *people* and *person* — often confuse writers. *People* is plural and pairs with plural pronouns:

> The people who scratched *their* names on the screen will be penalized.

Person is singular, as is any pronoun referring to *person*:

> The person who left *his or her* chewing gum on the computer screen is in big trouble.

WARNING

If you're writing a sentence similar to the preceding example, you may be tempted to match *their* with person. Resist the temptation. In Grammar World, singular and plural don't mingle, at least not legally.

Many people fall into this trap because they think "his or her" is cumbersome but they're afraid to choose just "his" or just "her." Later in the chapter, in the section "Avoiding Sexist Pronouns," I explain your options for making a word choice in this situation that won't earn you the label "sexist."

Getting Possessive with Your Pronouns

Possessive pronouns — those all-important words that indicate who owns what — also have singular and plural forms. You need to keep them straight. Table 3-2 helps you identify each type.

WARNING

The stickiest issues with possessive pronouns center around four pairs of words: *your/you're, their/they're, whose/who's,* and *its/it's.* Because creating the possessive form of a noun involves adding an apostrophe plus *s* to the end of the word (think *the lion's paw* or *the cat's meow*), many people assume that their possessive pronouns should contain apostrophes as well. As I detail in Chapter 9, that assumption will get you in serious trouble. Using *you're, they're, who's,* or *it's* as possessive pronouns is just plain wrong (and can cause fits among us grammatical types).

TABLE 3-2 **Singular and Plural Possessive Pronouns**

Singular	Plural
my	our
mine	ours
your	your
yours	yours
his	their/theirs
her	their
hers	theirs
its	their
whose	whose

Keeping Your Pronouns and Antecedents Close

One way to lose a reader is to let your pronouns wander far from the words they refer to — their antecedents. To avoid confusion, keep a pronoun and its antecedent near each other. Often, but not always, they appear in the same sentence. Sometimes they're in different sentences. Either way, the idea is the same: If the antecedent of the pronoun is too far away, the reader or listener may become confused. Check out this example:

> Bernie picked up the discarded *paper*. Enemy ships were all around, and the periscope's lenses were blurry. The sonar pings sounded like a Mozart sonata, and the captain's hangnails were acting up again. Yet even in the midst of such troubles, Bernie was neat. *It* made the deck look messy.

It? What's the meaning of *it?* You almost have to be an FBI decoder to find the noun partner of *it* (paper). Try the paragraph again:

> Enemy ships were all around, and the periscope's lenses were blurry. The sonar pings sounded like a Mozart sonata, and the

captain's hangnails were acting up again. Yet even in the midst of such troubles, Bernie was neat. He picked up the discarded *paper. It* made the deck look messy.

Now the antecedent and pronoun are next to each other. Much better!

Some people believe that position alone is enough to explain a pronoun-antecedent pairing. It's true that a pronoun is more likely to be understood if it's placed near the word it represents. In fact, you should form your sentences so that the pairs are neighbors. However, position isn't always enough to clarify the meaning of a pronoun. Standardized test writers want to know whether you can write clearly and express exact meaning, so they hit you with quite a few pronoun-antecedent problems.

The best way to clarify the meaning of a pronoun is to make sure that only one easily identifiable antecedent may be represented by each pronoun. If your sentence is about two females, don't use *she*. Instead, provide an extra noun to clarify your meaning.

Look at this sentence:

> Helena told her mother that she was out of cash.

Who is out of cash? The sentence has one pronoun — *she* — and two females *(Helena, her mother). She* could refer to either of the two nouns.

The rule here is simple: Be sure that your sentence has a clear, understandable pronoun-antecedent pair. If you can interpret the sentence in more than one way, rewrite it, using one or more sentences until your meaning is clear:

> Helena said, *"Mom,* can I have your ATM card? I looked in the cookie jar and *you're* out of cash."

or

> Helena saw that her mother was out of cash and told her so.

Question: What does the following sentence mean?

> Alexander and his brother went to Arthur's birthday party, but he didn't have a good time.

A. Alexander didn't have a good time.

B. Alexander's brother didn't have a good time.

C. Arthur didn't have a good time.

Answer: Who knows? Rewrite the sentence, unless you're talking to someone who was actually at the party and knows that Arthur got dumped by his girlfriend just before his chickenpox rash erupted and the cops arrived. If your listener knows all that, the sentence is fine. If not, here are a few possible rewrites:

> Alexander and his brother went to Arthur's birthday party. Arthur didn't have a good time.

or

> Arthur didn't have a good time at his own birthday party, even though Alexander and his brother attended.

or

> Alexander and his brother went to Arthur's birthday party, but Arthur didn't have a good time.

Pairing Pronouns with Pronoun Antecedents

Most of the time, determining whether a pronoun should be singular or plural is easy. Just check the noun that acts as the antecedent, and bingo, you're done. But sometimes a pronoun takes the place of another pronoun. The pronouns being replaced are particularly confusing because they're singular yet they look plural. In this section I tackle the hard cases, showing you how to handle these tricky pronouns when they're antecedents. (The same pronouns sometimes cause problems with subject-verb agreement; see Chapter 2.)

Wrestling with everybody, somebody, and no one

Everybody, somebody, and *no one* (not to mention *nothing* and *everyone*): These words should be barred from the English language. Why? Because matching these pronouns to other pronouns is a problem. If you match correctly, your choices sound wrong. But if you match incorrectly, you sound right. Sigh.

REMEMBER

Here's the deal. All of these pronouns are singular:

>> The *ones:* one, everyone, someone, anyone, no one

>> The *things:* everything, something, anything, nothing

>> The *bodies:* everybody, somebody, anybody, nobody

These pronouns don't sound singular. *Everybody* and *everyone* appear to represent a crowd. Nevertheless, you're in singular territory with these pronouns. The logic (yes, logic actually applies) is that *everyone* talks about the members of a group one by one. You follow this logic, probably unconsciously, when you choose a verb. You don't say,

> Everyone are here. Let the party begin!

Instead, you say,

> Everyone is here. Let the party begin!

WARNING

Picking the correct verb comes naturally, but picking the correct pronoun doesn't. Check out this pair:

> Everyone was asked to bring their bubble gum to the bubble-popping contest.

> Everyone was asked to bring his or her bubble gum to the bubble-popping contest.

Which one sounds right? The first one, I bet. Unfortunately, the second one is correct, formal English. The bottom line: When you need to refer to *ones, things,* or *bodies* in formal English, choose singular pronouns to match *(he/she, his/her)* and avoid using *their.*

Following each and every rule

Each and every time I explain this rule, someone objects. As with *everybody*, the proper use of *each* and *every* sounds wrong. These two pronouns are singular, and any pronouns that refer to *each* and *every* must also be singular. Check out these examples, in which I've italicized the pronouns referring to *each* and *every*:

> Each of the motorcycles should have *its* tires checked.
>
> Every motorcycle with leaky tires will have *its* inspection sticker removed.
>
> Every car, truck, and motorcycle on the road must display *its* inspection sticker on the windshield.
>
> Each of the owners must repair *his or her* motorcycle immediately.

Did you groan? Are you arguing with me? I understand. But I can't change the rule, which is based on the idea that *each* and *every* separate the members of the group into components. Any pronoun referring to *each* and *every* is actually referring to a member of the group, not to the group as a whole. Hence, you're in singular territory.

Examining either and neither

These two pronouns sometimes share a sentence with *or* and *nor*. But in this section I don't deal with *either/or* and *neither/nor* combos. For advice on handling that sort of sentence, turn to Chapter 5. Here I talk about *either* and *neither* alone, when these pronouns — and any pronouns referring to them — are always singular.

In the following sentences, the pronouns that refer to *either* and *neither* are italicized:

> Either of my daughters is willing to shave *her* head.
>
> Neither of the drill sergeants wants to deal with *his* fear of bald women.
>
> Either of the commanders must issue *his or her* order regulating hair length.

By the way, the last sentence assumes that you have a male and a female commander, or that you don't know whether the commanders are male, female, or a mixed pair. For more information on avoiding sexist pronouns, check out the next section.

Avoiding Sexist Pronouns

In preparing to write this section, I typed "pronoun + gender" into a Web search engine and then clicked "search." I wanted a tidbit or two from the Internet about the use of nonsexist language. I got more than a tidbit. In fact, I got more than 7 *million* hits. I can't believe that so many people are talking about pronouns! Actually, *talking* is not the appropriate word. *Arguing, warring, facing off, cursing,* and a few other less polite terms come to mind.

Here's the problem: For many years, the official rule was that masculine terms (those that refer to men) could refer to men only or could be universal, referring to both men and women. This rule is referred to as the *masculine universal.* For example, in an all-female gym class the teacher would say,

> Everyone must bring *her* gym shorts tomorrow.

and in an all-male gym class the teacher would say,

> Everyone must bring *his* gym shorts tomorrow.

Employing the masculine universal, in a mixed male-and-female gym class, the teacher would say,

> Everyone must bring *his* gym shorts tomorrow.

TIP

Judging by the Internet, the battles over this pronoun issue aren't likely to be over in the near future. My advice? I think you should say *he or she* and *his or her* when grammar requires such terms. The masculine universal excludes females and may offend your audience. However, if you're writing a longer work and find my suggestion cumbersome, consider your audience and decide whether using *he/his/him* or *she/her* throughout would be acceptable.

To sum up, if you need a pronoun (or pronouns) to refer to both men and women, you may say,

Everyone must bring *his or her* gym shorts tomorrow.

or

All the students must bring *their* gym shorts tomorrow.

or

Bring *your* gym shorts tomorrow, *you* little creeps!

All these examples are grammatically correct and allow you to avoid the masculine universal.

IN THIS CHAPTER

» **Identifying the elements of a complete sentence**

» **Eliminating sentence fragments and run-ons**

» **Uniting two or more complete sentences properly**

» **Joining ideas of unequal importance**

» **Gluing sentences together with pronouns**

» **Avoiding the danglers**

Chapter **4**

Constructing a Complete Sentence

Everyone knows the most important rule of English grammar: All sentences must be complete. But everyone breaks the rule. I just did! *But everyone breaks the rule* is not a complete sentence; it's a sentence *fragment*. At times, fragments are acceptable, and in this chapter I explain when you can get away with writing one. The other extreme — more than one complete sentence improperly glued together — is a *run-on sentence*. Run-on sentences and their variation, *comma splices*, are never okay. In fact, they're grammatical felonies.

Never fear: In this chapter I explain all the ins and outs of joining ideas together in a sentence without risking a visit from the Grammar Police.

Creating Complete Sentences from Complete Thoughts

In this section, I spell out the required elements for any complete sentence: a subject-verb pair and a complete thought. Often, to achieve a complete thought, a sentence requires one or more complements (no, I don't mean you must praise the sentence for its lovely verbs. That would be a *compliment*). I explain the four types of complements here as well.

Locating subject-verb pairs

A complete sentence has at least one subject-verb pair. If you can't find a subject and a verb that belong together (a topic I discuss in Chapter 2), you don't have a complete sentence.

Complete sentences may include more than one subject-verb pair:

> Dorothy fiddled while the orchestra pit burned. (*Dorothy* = subject of the verb *fiddled; orchestra pit* = subject of the verb *burned*)

> Not only did George swim, but he also sipped the pool water. (*George* = subject of the verb *did swim; he* = subject of the verb *sipped*)

As I note in Chapter 2, complete sentences may also match one subject with more than one verb, and vice versa:

> The lizard with a British accent appeared in three commercials but sang in only two. (*lizard* = subject of the verbs *appeared* and *sang*)

> Alice and Archie will fight endlessly over a single birdseed. (*Alice* and *Archie* = subjects of the verb *will fight*)

In some cases, you can infer the subject of a sentence without seeing it. Complete sentences that give commands may match an understood subject (you) with the verb:

> Give me a coupon. (*you-understood* = subject of the verb *give*)

If you need a refresher on you-understood, you can find it in Chapter 2 as well.

TIP

Not relying on context

A complete sentence must express a complete thought. Here are a couple examples of incomplete thoughts:

> The reason I wanted a divorce was.

> Because I said so.

Granted, both examples may be part of a longer conversation, which means that in context, these incomplete thoughts may express a complete thought:

> Sydney: So the topic of conversation was the Rangers' season opener?
> Alice: No! The reason I wanted a divorce was!

and

> Sydney: Why do I have to do this dumb homework?
> Alice: Because I said so.

You can pull a complete thought out of these examples, but a conversation's context isn't enough to satisfy the complete thought/complete sentence rule. To be legal, your sentence must express a complete thought without considering context.

WARNING

In deciding whether you have a complete sentence, you may be led astray by words that resemble questions. Consider the words *who knits well*. A complete thought? Maybe, maybe not. Suppose these three words form a question:

> Who knits well?

This question is understandable, and its thought is complete. But suppose these three words form a statement:

> Who knits well.

Now they don't make sense. This incomplete sentence needs more words to make a complete thought.

Occasionally, a complete sentence ends with an *ellipsis:* three spaced dots (. . .). Such sentences often show up in dramatic works to add suspense or to indicate hesitation or confusion. These sentences appear incomplete, but because they fulfill the author's purpose, they *are* complete. For more on ellipses, see "Getting your endmarks in place" later in the chapter.

Fishing for complements

Complements are parts of a sentence that are often — but not always — required to create a complete thought. Four kinds of complements show up in sentences: direct objects, indirect objects, object complements, and subject complements. If you never learn their names, that's fine; the following information simply shows you the role these sentence finishers play in helping you create complete thoughts.

Receiving the action: Direct objects

Imagine that you throw a baseball and it crashes through the picture window in your living room. Your mother yells from the kitchen, "What's going on?" You mutter something containing the word *broke.* (There's the verb.) "Who broke something?" she demands. You concede that *you* did. (There's the subject.) "What did you break?" You confess: *the picture window.* (There's the complement.)

> You broke the picture window!

Broke is an action verb because it tells you what happened. The action comes from the subject *(you)* and goes to an object *(the window). The window* receives the action expressed by the verb *broke.* Conclusion? *Window* is a *direct object* because it receives the action directly from the verb.

TIP

You can recognize direct objects more easily if you think of them as part of a pattern in the sentence structure: subject (S)-action verb (AV)-direct object (DO). This S-AV-DO pattern is one of the most common in the English language.

A sentence can have more than one direct object. Check out these examples:

> Al autographed *posters* and *books* for his many admirers.

> Roger will eat a dozen *doughnuts* and a few *slabs* of cheesecake for breakfast.

And some sentences have no direct object:

> Throughout the endless afternoon and into the lonely night, Al sighed sadly.

No one or nothing receives the sighs, so the sentence has no direct object. Perhaps that's why Al is lonely.

Rare, but sometimes there: Indirect objects

Another type of complement is the *indirect object*. Why *indirect*? Because the action of the verb doesn't flow directly to it. (I just wrote a fragment. Did you catch that?) This complement is sort of an intermediary between the action verb and the direct object.

> Knowing that I'm on a diet, my former friend sent *me* six dozen chocolates.

The action is *sent*. My former *friend* performed the action, so *friend* is the subject. What received the action? Six dozen *chocolates*. *Chocolates* is the direct object; it received the action of the verb directly. But *me* also received the action, indirectly. *Me* received the sending of the boxes of chocolate. *Me* is the indirect object.

TIP

The sentence pattern for indirect objects is subject (S)–action verb (AV)–indirect object (IO)–direct object (DO). The indirect object always precedes the direct object. In these examples, the indirect objects are italicized:

> Gloria will tell *me* the whole story tomorrow. (*will tell* = verb, *Gloria* = subject, and *story* = direct object)

> Ella sent *Larry* a sharp message. (*sent* = verb, *Ella* = subject, and *message* = direct object)

REMEMBER

Indirect objects don't appear very often. When they do show up, they're always in partnership with a direct object. You probably don't need to worry about knowing the difference between direct and indirect objects (unless you're an English teacher). As long as you understand that these words complete the meaning of an action verb, you recognize the basic composition of a sentence.

No bias here: Object complements

Sometimes a direct object doesn't get the whole job done. A little more information is needed (or just desired), and the writer doesn't want to bother adding a new subject-verb pair. The solution? An *object complement*: an added fact about the direct object.

The object complement (italicized in the following sentences) may be a person, place, or thing. In other words, it may be a noun:

> Gloria and others with her worldview elected Roger *president*. (*elected* = verb, *Gloria and others* = subject, and *Roger* = direct object)

> Al called his dog *Al-Too*. (*called* = verb, *Al* = subject, and *dog* = direct object)

The object complement may also be an *adjective*, a word that describes a noun (see Chapter 6):

> Nancy considered her *lazy* at best. (*considered* = verb, *Nancy* = subject, and *her* = direct object)

> Roger called George *heartless*. (*called* = verb, *Roger* = subject, and *George* = direct object)

The object complement in each sample sentence gives the sentence an extra jolt. You know more with it than you do without it.

Finishing the equation: Subject complements

Subject complements are major players in sentences. A *linking verb* (see Chapter 2) begins a word equation; it expresses a state of being, linking two ideas. The complement completes the equation. Because a complement following a linking verb expresses something about the *subject* of the sentence, it's called a *subject complement*. In each of the following sentences, the first idea is the subject, and the second idea (italicized) is the complement:

> Nerdo is *upset* by the bankruptcy of the pocket-protector manufacturer. *(Nerdo = upset)*

> Gloria was a *cheerleader* before the dog bite incident. *(Gloria = cheerleader)*

> It is *I*, the master of the universe. *(It = I)*

Subject complements can take several forms. Sometimes the subject complement is a descriptive word (an *adjective*), and sometimes it's a *noun* (person, place, thing, or idea) or a *pronoun* (a word that substitutes for a noun).

WARNING

You can't mix types of subject complements in the same sentence, completing the meaning of the same verb. Use all descriptions (adjectives) or all nouns and pronouns. Take a look at these examples:

> **Wrong:** Gramps is grouchy and a patron of the arts.

> **Right:** Gramps is a grouch and a patron of the arts.

> **Also right:** Gramps is grouchy and arty.

Banning Fragments from Formal Writing

I use incomplete sentences, or *fragments*, here and there throughout this book, and (I hope) these incomplete sentences aren't confusing. People today are much more comfortable with fragments than our elderly relatives were. Chances are you use fragments frequently when you text or write e-mails. If you're writing for an audience that doesn't demand formal English, fragments that communicate their message clearly may work just fine.

The most common type of fragment uses the words *and, or, but*, or *nor*. These words are *conjunctions*, and as I explain in "Attaching Sentences Legally" later in this chapter, these conjunctions may combine two complete sentences (with two complete thoughts) into one longer sentence:

> Eggworthy went to his doctor for a cholesterol check, *and* then he scrambled home.

Nowadays, more and more writers begin sentences with *and, or, but*, and *nor*, especially in informal writing or for dramatic effect. For example, the preceding sentence may be turned into

> Eggworthy went to his doctor for a cholesterol check. And then he scrambled home.

The second sentence is now a fragment.

Beginning sentences with *and, or, but,* and *nor* is still not acceptable in formal English grammar. If you see a sentence beginning with one of these words in the error-recognition portion of a standardized test, consider it a fragment. When you're writing an essay, you should also avoid fragments.

WARNING

Another common error is to write a fragment that lacks a complete thought. This sort of fragment usually begins with a subordinate conjunction (see "Making connections with subordinate conjunctions" later in this chapter). Here are two examples of this type of sentence fragment:

> As if he were king of the world.

> Whether you like it or not, although I am really sorry that you are upset.

TIP

Don't let the number of words in sentence fragments fool you. As these examples show, some sentence fragments are short, and some aren't. Decide by meaning, not by length.

Enough Is Enough: Avoiding Run-ons

While fragments are becoming more acceptable in informal writing (as long as they don't create confusion), run-ons are never okay because they always muddy your meaning and leave your reader gasping for breath.

In this section, I show you how to avoid run-ons by properly punctuating the ends of your sentences. I then introduce a common variety of the run-on — the *comma splice* — and show some simple fixes that eradicate it.

Getting your endmarks in place

When you speak, your body language, silences, and tone act as punctuation marks. You wriggle your eyebrows, stop at significant moments, and raise your tone when you ask a question. When you write, you can't raise an eyebrow or stop for a dramatic moment. No one hears your tone of voice, so grammar uses endmarks.

You need endmarks to close your sentences legally. Without them, you create run-ons and confuse your reader. The endmarks you use most often are the period (.), question mark (?), and exclamation point (!). The following examples show how to use these endmarks to avoid run-ons.

The period is for ordinary statements, declarations, and commands:

> **The run-on:** I can't do my homework it's too difficult
>
> **The fix:** I can't do my homework. It's too difficult.

The question mark is (shockingly) for questions:

> **The run-on:** Why are you torturing me with this homework can't you just leave me alone
>
> **The fix:** Why are you torturing me with this homework? Can't you just leave me alone?

The exclamation point adds a little drama to sentences that would otherwise end in periods:

> **The run-on:** Oh, the agony of homework I've seen it's enough to make a grown man cry
>
> **The fix:** Oh, the agony of homework I've seen! It's enough to make a grown man cry!

A fourth type of endmark — used less frequently than the others — is an *ellipsis* (. . .). The three dots signal that something has been left out of a sentence. (When missing words occur at the end of a sentence, you actually use four dots: one for the period at the end of the sentence and three for the missing words.) For example,

> Michael choked, "I can't do my. . . ."

No matter how much you fear run-ons, don't put more than one endmark at the end of a sentence unless you're trying to create a comic effect:

> He said my cooking tasted like what?!?!?!

Fixing comma splices

A *comma spice* is a run-on in which a comma attempts to unite two complete thoughts:

> Abner will clip the thorns from that rose stem, he is afraid of scratching himself.

Fixing a comma splice isn't tough; you either have to allow the thoughts to remain separate or identify a legal way to combine them. The following examples show that using a proper endmark (a period) after the first sentence is one option, and replacing the comma with a semicolon is another:

> Abner will clip the thorns from that rose stem. He is afraid of scratching himself.

> Abner will clip the thorns from that rose stem; he is afraid of scratching himself.

Keep reading to find out why a semicolon is stronger than a comma and to discover lots more ways to combine complete thoughts legally.

Attaching Sentences Legally

TEST ALERT

Standardized test-makers enjoy plopping run-on sentences and comma splices into paragraphs and checking whether you can identify the run-ons as grammatically incorrect. Teachers who score the writing section of the SAT also frown on run-ons and comma splices. The best way to avoid this type of grammar error is to figure out how to connect sentences legally, as I detail in this section.

Employing coordinate conjunctions

Coordinate conjunctions — *and, but, or, nor, for, so,* and *yet* — are little powerhouses that join words or longer expressions together. They're strong enough to join complete sentences, and they may also unite all sorts of equal grammatical elements. Here they are in action, joining complete sentences:

The rain pelted Abner's gray hair, *and* his green velvet shoes were completely ruined.

The CEO told Tanya to text the address of the restaurant to everyone, *but* Tanya had no idea where the restaurant was.

You can take a hike, *or* you can jump off a cliff.

Ben did not know how to shoe a horse, *nor* did he understand equine psychology.

The townspeople lined the streets, *for* they had heard a rumor about Lady Godiva.

The coordinate conjunctions give equal emphasis to the elements they join. In the preceding sentences, the ideas on one side of the conjunction have no more importance than the ideas on the other side of the conjunction.

When the conjunctions *and, but, or, nor,* and *for* unite two complete sentences, a comma precedes the conjunction. For the lowdown on commas, turn to Chapter 7.

Some words appear to be strong enough to join sentences, but in reality they're just a bunch of 98-pound weaklings. False joiners include *however, consequently, therefore, moreover, also,* and *furthermore.* Use these words to add meaning to your sentences but not to glue the sentences together. When you see these words on a standardized exam, be careful! A favorite test-maker trick is to plop these words into a run-on:

Run on: Levon gobbled the birdseed, consequently, Robbie had nothing to eat.

Corrected version #1: Levon gobbled the birdseed; consequently, Robbie had nothing to eat.

Corrected version #2: Levon gobbled the birdseed. Consequently, Robbie had nothing to eat.

Notice the semicolon in the first corrected sentence? Semicolons are equivalent to coordinate conjunctions. According to the Official Grammarian's Rule Book (which doesn't exist), semicolons can join two complete sentences under certain conditions. See the next section for details.

Relying on semicolons

The semicolon (;) is a funny little punctuation mark; it functions as a pit stop between one idea and another. It's not as strong as a period, but a semicolon lets the reader take a rest — just for a moment. This punctuation mark is strong enough to attach one complete sentence to another.

I've seen writing manuals that proclaim, "Never use semicolons!" with the same intensity of feeling as, say, "Don't blow up the world with that nuclear missile!" Other people can't get enough of them. As far as I'm concerned, use them if you like them, or ignore them if you don't.

REMEMBER

If you do put a semicolon in your sentence, be sure to attach related ideas. Here's an example:

Right: Grover was born in Delaware; he moved to Virginia when he was 4.

Wrong: I put nonfat yogurt into that soup; I like Stephen King's books.

In the first example, both parts of the sentence are about Grover's living arrangements. In the second, the two ideas are, to put it mildly, not in the same universe.

Connecting Unequal Ideas

In the average company, the boss runs the show. The boss has subordinates who play two important roles: They must do at least some work, and they must make the boss feel like the center of the universe. Leave the boss alone in the office, and everything's fine. Leave the employees alone in the office, and pretty soon someone is swinging from the light fixture.

Some sentences resemble companies. The "boss" part of a sentence is all right by itself; it expresses a complete thought. The "employee" can't stand alone; it's an incomplete thought. In case you're into grammar lingo, the boss is an *independent clause,* and the employee is a *dependent* or *subordinate clause.*

WARNING

Independent clauses are okay by themselves, but putting too many in a row makes your writing choppy and monotonous. Subordinate clauses are never okay by themselves because they're sentence fragments. Together, the boss and the employee create more powerful sentences. Check out two examples:

> **Boss:** Jack ate the bagel.
>
> **Employee:** after he had picked out all the raisins.
>
> **Joining 1:** Jack ate the bagel after he had picked out all the raisins.
>
> **Joining 2:** After he had picked out all the raisins, Jack ate the bagel.
>
> **Boss:** The book bag is in the garage.
>
> **Employee:** that Larry lost
>
> **Joining:** The book bag that Larry lost is in the garage.

The joined example sentences are grammatically legal because they contain at least one complete thought, which can stand on its own as a complete sentence.

Giving subordinate clauses a job

Okay, so subordinate clauses can't stand alone. What can they do? They have three main purposes in life, as you see in the following sections.

Describing nouns and pronouns

A subordinate clause may give your listener or reader more information about a noun or pronoun in the sentence. Here are some examples, with the subordinate clause in italics:

> The book *that Michael wrote* is on the bestseller list. (*that Michael wrote* describes the noun *book*.)
>
> Anyone *who knows Michael well* will read the book. (*who knows Michael well* describes the pronoun *anyone*.)

Describing verbs, adjectives, or adverbs

Subordinate clauses can also describe verbs, adjectives, or adverbs. These subordinate clauses tell you *how, when, where,* or *why:*

> We will probably find out more when the movie version is released. (*when the movie version is released* describes the verb *will find.*)

> Michael is so stubborn that he may sue the government. (*that he may sue the government* describes the adverb *so.*)

Acting as subjects or objects inside another clause

This function is a bit more complicated: Subordinate clauses may do any job that a noun does in a sentence. Subordinate clauses sometimes act as a subject or object inside another clause. Here are some examples:

> *When the book was written* is a real mystery. (*When the book was written* is the subject of the verb *is.*)

> Michael signed copies for *whoever bought at least five books.* (*whoever bought at least five books* is the object of the preposition *for.*)

Finding homes for your subordinate clauses

Correctly placing your subordinate clauses is simple. Clauses acting as subjects or objects nearly always fall in the proper place automatically. Don't worry about them!

Put a subordinate clause that describes a noun or pronoun near the word that it describes. Here are a few examples of proper placement of clauses that describe nouns and pronouns:

> Larry's wedding coordinator took care of every detail; he even baked the cakes *that Larry's guests enjoyed.* (The italicized clause describes the noun *cakes.*)

> Anyone *who is on a diet* should stay away from Larry's weddings. (The italicized clause describes the pronoun *anyone.*)

A subordinate clause that describes the verb usually lands at the front or rear of the sentence:

> *Although Anna understood the equation,* she chose to put a question mark on her answer sheet. (The italicized clause describes the verb *chose.*)

> She wrote the question mark *because she wanted to make a statement about the mysteries of life.* (The italicized clause describes the verb *wrote.*)

Making connections with subordinate conjunctions

The conjunctions in the boss–employee type of sentence do double duty: They emphasize that one idea is more important than the other, and they give some information about the relationship between the two ideas. These conjunctions are called *subordinate conjunctions.* Some common subordinate conjunctions are *while, because, although, though, since, when, where, if, whether, before, until, than, as, as if, in order that, so that, whenever,* and *wherever.* (Whew!)

Check out how conjunctions are used in these examples:

Sentence 1: Michael was shaving. (not a very important activity)

Sentence 2: The earthquake destroyed the city. (a rather important event)

If you join these two sentences as equals with a coordinate conjunction (see the earlier section "Employing coordinate conjunctions"), you emphasize both events:

Michael was shaving, *and* the earthquake destroyed the city.

Grammatically, the sentence is legal. Morally, this statement poses a problem. Is Michael's avoidance of five o'clock shadow equal in importance to an earthquake that measures 7 on the Richter scale? Better to join these clauses as unequals with the help of a subordinate conjunction, making the main idea about the earthquake the boss:

While Michael was shaving, the earthquake destroyed the city.

or

> The earthquake destroyed the city *while* Michael was shaving.

The *while* gives you time information, attaches the employee sentence to the boss sentence, and shows the greater importance of the earthquake. Not bad for five letters.

Here's another:

Sentence 1: Esther must do her homework now.

Sentence 2: Mom is on the warpath.

In combining these two ideas, you have decisions to make. If you put them together as equals, the reader will wonder why you're mentioning both statements at the same time:

> Esther must do her homework now, *but* Mom is on the warpath.

This joining may mean that Mom is running around the house screaming at the top of her lungs. Esther finds that concentrating is impossible during Mom's tantrums and won't get anything done until Mom settles down with a cup of tea. That's one possible meaning of this joined sentence. But why leave your reader guessing? Try another joining:

> Esther must do her homework now *because* Mom is on the warpath.

This sentence is much clearer: Esther's mother got a note from the teacher. Esther knows that if she wants to survive through high school graduation, she'd better get to work now. One more joining to check:

> Mom is on the warpath *because* Esther must do her homework now.

In this version, Esther's mother has asked her daughter to clean the garage. She's been asking Esther every day for the last two years. But Esther told her that she couldn't clean up now because she had to do her homework. World War III erupted immediately.

Do you see the power of these joining words? These conjunctions strongly influence sentence meaning.

Combining Sentences with Pronouns

A useful trick for combining short sentences legally is "the pronoun connection." (A *pronoun* substitutes for a noun; see Chapter 3.) *That, which,* and *who* are the pronouns you use, and they serve as thumbtacks, attaching a subordinate or less important idea to the main body of the sentence.

Check out this combination:

> **Sentence 1:** Amy read the book.
>
> **Sentence 2:** The book had a thousand pictures in it.
>
> **Joining:** Amy read the book *that* had a thousand pictures in it.

In the joined sentence, *that* takes the place of the noun *book.* You use *that* because the clause *(had a thousand pictures in it)* is essential to the reader's understanding of the sentence; without it, the reader has no idea which book Amy read. If the clause were nonessential, you'd use *which* (preceded by a comma) instead, as in the following example:

> **Sentence 1:** The paper map stuck to Wilbur's shoe.
>
> **Sentence 2:** We plan to use the map to take over the world.
>
> **Joining:** The paper map, *which* we plan to use to take over the world, stuck to Wilbur's shoe.

Readers may be thrilled to know that you'll be using the map to take over the world, but even without that added information, they still know which map you're talking about (the paper one that's stuck to Wilbur's shoe).

When does *who* come into play? When the noun being replaced is a person:

> **Sentence 1:** Margaret wants to hire a carpenter.
>
> **Sentence 2:** The carpenter will build a new ant farm for her pets.
>
> **Joining:** Margaret wants to hire a carpenter *who* will build a new ant farm for her pets.

Don't Keep Your Audience Hanging: Removing Danglers

WARNING

One way to foul up an otherwise complete sentence is to describe something that isn't there. Two particular types of descriptions tend to cause as many problems as a double date with your ex: participles and infinitives. These descriptions look like verbs but don't function as verbs.

In this section, I show you common mistakes that writers make with participles and infinitives. Don't worry about the grammatical terms; you don't need to know them. Just focus on the examples I provide for placing descriptions properly.

Dangling participles

Read this sentence:

> Munching a buttered sausage, the cholesterol really builds up.

The sentence begins with a verb form, *munching*, but *munching* isn't the verb in the sentence. It's a *participle:* a verb form that describes. (The verb in the sentence is *builds*.) Participles have to describe something or someone, so *munching* must be tacked onto a muncher. Who is munching in this sentence? Unfortunately, no one is munching.

Descriptive verb forms that have nothing appropriate to describe are called *danglers* or *dangling modifiers*. To correct the sentence, add a muncher:

> Munching a buttered sausage, Eggworthy smiled and waved to his cardiologist.

REMEMBER

In sentences beginning with a descriptive verb form, such as a participle, the subject must perform the action mentioned in the descriptive verb form. In the sample sentence, Eggworthy is the subject. The sentence begins with a descriptive verb form, *munching a buttered sausage*. Thus, Eggworthy is the one who is munching. If you want the cardiologist to munch, say

> Munching a buttered sausage, the cardiologist returned Eggworthy's wave.

Here's another problematic example:

> Sitting on the park bench, the soaring space shuttle briefly delighted the little boy.

Oh, really? The space shuttle is sitting on a bench and soaring at the same time? Defies the laws of physics, don't you think? Try again:

> Sitting on the park bench, the little boy was briefly delighted by the soaring space shuttle.

Now *little boy* is the subject, so the introductory description applies to him, not to the space shuttle.

This topic is so popular on the SAT that it deserves another example. Here's a faulty sentence:

> Skidding over the icy pavement, the old oak tree couldn't escape the speeding sports car.

You spotted the problem, right? The *tree* is the subject of the sentence, but a tree can't be the thing *skidding over the icy pavement*. That sort of thing happens only in Harry Potter movies. Now for the better version:

> Skidding over the icy pavement, the speeding sports car slammed into the old oak tree.

Now the *speeding sports car* is skidding. No problem. Well, no grammar problem anyway.

Dangling infinitives

Another common dangler is an *infinitive* (*to* + a verb) that begins a sentence.

> To sew well, a strong light is necessary.

This sentence may sound correct to you, but think about the meaning for a moment. Who is sewing? No one, at least the way the sentence is now written. Moving the infinitive may make the sentence sound better to your ears, but the move doesn't solve the problem:

> A strong light is necessary to sew well.

There's still no one sewing, so the sentence is still incorrect. To fix the problem, you must add a person:

> To sew well, you need a strong light. (*You* are sewing.)

> To sew well, sit near a strong light. (*You* is understood in this command sentence.)

An infinitive at the beginning of a sentence *may* be legal. Check out this sentence:

> To sew well is Betsy's goal.

In this sentence, *to sew well* isn't a description; it's an activity. In other words, *to sew well* is the subject in this sentence. How do you tell the difference between a subject and a description? A subject pairs with a verb (*is* in the example sentence) and answers the question *who?* or *what?* (For help finding the subject of a sentence, turn to Chapter 2.) A description is an add-on, contributing more information about something else in the sentence.

Chapter 5

Drawing Parallels (Without the Lines)

I n math class, you plot parallels on a graph. In grammar, you create parallel constructions. When I say *parallel constructions*, I'm not talking about lines that look like train tracks. I'm talking about the need for balance in speech and writing — the need to create sentences that aren't lopsided. I'm talking about the reason Hamlet says, "To be or not to be" instead of "Being or not to be." In this chapter, I show you how to avoid everyday errors of parallelism — what hard-hatted grammarians call *faulty construction*.

TEST ALERT

If you're of test-taking age, be aware that parallelism plays a starring role in the SAT but is less important on the ACT. Why? I have no idea. Maybe one of the SAT writers was mugged by an unparallel sentence during childhood.

Seeking Balance

Can you spot the problem in this sentence?

Larry wanted with all his heart to find a bride who was smart, beautiful, and had millions of dollars.

Aside from Larry's unrealistic matrimonial notions, the sentence has another problem: It's not parallel. Concentrate on the part of the sentence following the word *was*. Larry's dream bride needed these characteristics:

>> Smart
>> Beautiful
>> Had millions of dollars

These three descriptions don't match. The first two are adjectives. The third consists of a verb (*had*) and an object (*millions of dollars*). (I cover adjectives in Chapter 6, verbs in Chapter 2, and objects in Chapter 4.) But all three descriptions are doing the same job in the sentence — describing Larry's dream bride. Because they're doing the same job, they should match, at least in the grammatical sense. Here's one revised list:

>> Smart
>> Beautiful
>> Rich

And here's another:

>> Intelligence
>> Beauty
>> Millions of dollars

Both lists are fine. In the first list, all the characteristics of Larry's bride are adjectives. In the second, all the characteristics are nouns. You can use either list; just don't take some elements from one and some from another. Here are the revised sentences:

Larry wanted with all his heart to find a bride who was smart, beautiful, and rich.

Larry wanted with all his heart to find a bride with intelligence, beauty, and millions of dollars.

REMEMBER

Parallelism is especially important when you're making a presentation or a bulleted list. If one item is a complete sentence, all the items should be. If you're listing nouns, make sure every item is a noun. For example, see if you can spot the error here:

This year's goals for employees of Kubla Khan, Inc. include the following:

- To visit the stately dome
- Rafting the sacred river Alph
- Locating a competent dulcimer player

Uh-oh. One item doesn't match: *to visit the stately dome.* Here's how the list appears to a grammarian: *to visit* is an infinitive (*to* + a verb), but the next two items, *rafting* and *locating,* are *gerunds* (verb forms that end in *-ing* and are used as nouns). Here are two possible corrections for the list:

>> Visiting the stately dome

>> Rafting the sacred river Alph

>> Locating a competent dulcimer player

or

>> To visit the stately dome

>> To go rafting on the sacred river Alph

>> To locate a competent dulcimer player

Check out another example:

> **Not parallel:** Anna said that whenever anything went wrong, whenever someone let us down, or in case of disaster, she would "feel our pain."

> **What's wrong:** The three things that Anna said are not parallel. Two have subject-verb combinations *(anything went, someone let),* and one *(in case of disaster)* does not.

> **Parallel:** Anna said that whenever anything went wrong, whenever someone let us down, or whenever disaster struck, she would "feel our pain."

> **Why it's parallel:** Now the three things that Anna said are all subject-verb combinations.

TIP

To avoid parallelism errors, you don't have to know the correct grammatical terms — just listen. A parallel sentence has balance. A nonparallel sentence doesn't.

Striving for Consistency

If you've ever ridden in a car with a stick shift, you know that smooth transitions are rare. If something is just a little off, the car bucks like a mule. The same thing is true in sentences. You can, at times, shift tense, voice, or person, but even the slightest mistake stalls your sentence. In this section, I explain how to avoid unnecessary shifts and how to check your sentences for consistency.

Matching verb tenses

Check out this sentence with multiple verbs:

> Larry begs Ella to marry him, offers her a crown and a private room, and finally won her hand.

Now make a list of the verbs in the sentence:

>> Begs

>> Offers

>> Won

The first two verbs are in present tense, but the third shifts into past tense for no valid reason. If the verbs in this sentence were gears in a stick shift, your car would conk out. All three verbs should be in present tense or past tense. Here are the corrected versions of the sentence:

> Larry begs Ella to marry him, offers her a crown and a private room, and finally wins her hand. (All three verbs are in present tense.)

or

> Larry begged Ella to marry him, offered her a crown and a private room, and finally won her hand. (All three verbs are in past tense.)

Sometimes in telling a story, you must shift tense because the story's action requires a change in time. For example:

> Betsy always *practices* for at least 10 hours a day, unless she *is giving* a concert. Last week she *flew* to Antarctica for a recital. When she *arrived,* the piano *was frozen.* Nevertheless, the show *went* on. Next week Betsy *will practice* 12 hours a day to make up for the time she *lost* last week.

Betsy's story has lots of verb tenses: present *(practices)*, present progressive *(is giving)*, past *(flew, arrived, was frozen, went, lost)*, and future *(will practice)*. Each change of tense is justified by the information in the story.

Here's an example of an unjustified shift in verb tense:

> **Wrong:** Max *slips* on the ice and, after obsessively checking every inch of his skull in the mirror, *decided* that he *had hurt* his head.

> **Why it's wrong:** The first verb is in present tense. The sentence shifts to past tense for no reason.

> **Right:** Max *slipped* on the ice and, after obsessively checking every inch of his skull in the mirror, *decided* that he *had hurt* his head.

Staying active (or passive)

The *voice* of a verb is either active or passive. In Chapter 11, I explain the difference between the two. Very briefly, a verb is passive if the subject of a sentence is the person or thing receiving an action. (For example, in *The cookies were baked by my grandmother,* the cookies receive the action of baking.) When the subject of a sentence is the person or thing doing the action, the verb is active. (For example, *My grandmother baked these cookies* conveys the same idea using an active verb.)

REMEMBER

Like tense, the voice of the verbs in a sentence should be consistent unless there's a good reason for a shift. Here's a sentence with an unjustified shift in voice:

> Larry *polished* the diamond engagement ring, *rechecked* the certificate of authenticity, and *was crushed* when his intended bride *said* no.

The problem may be hard to spot, but a checklist of the verbs can help:

- ❯❯ Polished
- ❯❯ Rechecked
- ❯❯ Was crushed
- ❯❯ Said

The first two verbs and the last one are in active voice, but the third is in passive voice.

A number of changes can take care of the problem, such as:

Larry *polished* the diamond engagement ring, *rechecked* the certificate of authenticity, and *cried* like a baby when his intended bride *said* no.

or

Larry *polished* the diamond engagement ring and *rechecked* the certificate of authenticity. His intended bride *crushed* him with her refusal.

REMEMBER

Notice that the verbs in the corrected sentences are all in active voice: *polished, rechecked, cried, said* and *polished, rechecked, crushed.* In general, active voice is better than passive. Listen to this clunker:

The diamond engagement ring was polished and the certificate of authenticity was rechecked by Larry, and Larry was crushed when "no" was said to him by his intended bride.

I don't think so. The passive verbs create a wordy mess.

Being true to your person

Ah, loyalty. It's one of the most celebrated virtues — in life as well as in grammar! Loyalty in grammar relates to what grammarians call *person*. In *first person*, the subject narrates the story; *I* or *we* acts as the subject of the sentence. In *second person*, the subject is being spoken to, and *you* (either singular or plural) is the subject.

In *third person*, the subject is being spoken about, using *he, she, it, they*, or any other word that talks *about* someone or something.

REMEMBER

To be loyal, don't start out a sentence talking from the point of view of one person and then switch to another point of view, unless you have a valid reason for doing so. Here's an example of an unnecessary shift in person:

> To celebrate his marriage, Larry gave every person in his kingdom the day off from work because you need to do something spectacular on such an important occasion.

The first part of the sentence talks about *Larry*, so it's in third person. The second part of the sentence, which begins with the word *because*, shifts to *you* (second person). Making the correction is simple:

> To celebrate his marriage, *Larry* gave every person in his kingdom the day off from work because *he* needs to do something spectacular on such an important occasion.

or

> To celebrate his marriage, *Larry* gave every person in his kingdom the day off from work because *everyone* needs to do something spectacular on such an important occasion.

In the first corrected sentence, *Larry* is the subject of the first part of the sentence, and *he* is the subject of the second part. No problem — both are in third person. In the second correction, *Larry* is matched with *everyone* (a third-person pronoun).

Time for another round:

> **Wrong:** *I* am going to pick up some of those coins; *you* can't pass up a chance for free money!
>
> **Why it's wrong:** The first part of the sentence is in first person *(I)*, and the second part shifts to *you*, the second-person form. Why shift?
>
> **Right:** *I* am going to pick up some of those coins; *I* can't pass up a chance for free money!

Using Conjunction Pairs Correctly

Most joining words (called *conjunctions*) fly solo. Single conjunctions — *and, but, nor, or, because, although, since,* and so on — join sentences or parts of sentences (see Chapter 4). Some joining words, however, come in pairs. Here are some of the most frequently used pairs:

>> Not only/but also

>> Either/or

>> Neither/nor

>> Whether/or

>> Both/and

REMEMBER

Some of these words show up in sentences without their partners. No problem! Just make sure that when they do act as conjunction pairs, they behave properly. Here's the rule: Whatever fills in the blanks after these pairs of conjunctions must have the same grammatical identity. The logic here is that conjunctions have partners, and so do the things they join. You may join two nouns, two prepositional phrases — two whatevers! Just make sure the things that you join match. Check out this example:

> Not only Larry but also his bride yearned for a day at the beach. (The conjunction pair joins two nouns, *Larry* and *his bride*.)
>
> Either you or I must break the news to Larry. (The conjunction pair joins two pronouns, *you* and *I*.)

REMEMBER

Nouns and pronouns are equals when it comes to parallelism. Because pronouns take the place of nouns, you may mix them:

> Neither Ralph nor he has brought a proper present to Larry's wedding. (The conjunction pair joins a noun, *Ralph*, and a pronoun, *he*.)

To help you spot parallelism errors in sentences with conjunction pairs, here are two mismatches and their corrections:

> **Not parallel:** Either *Lulu will go with Larry to the bachelor party* or *to the shower*, but she won't attend both.

Why it's not parallel: The first italicized section is a subject-verb combination, but the second is a prepositional phrase.

Parallel: Lulu will go with Larry either *to the bachelor party* or *to the shower,* but she won't attend both. (Now you have two prepositional phrases.)

Not parallel: Both *her lateness* and *that she was dressed in white leather* insulted the royal couple.

Why it's not parallel: The first italicized section is a noun, but the second is a subject-verb combination.

Parallel but a little repetitive: Both *the fact that she was late* and *the fact that she was dressed in white leather* insulted the royal couple. (Now the italicized sections are both subject-verb combinations.)

Parallel: Both *her lateness* and *her white leather clothing* insulted the royal couple. (Now the italicized sections are both nouns with a few descriptions tossed in — a more concise solution.)

Constructing Proper Comparisons

WARNING

The Grammar Police will arrive, warrant in hand, if your comparisons aren't parallel. Comparisons to watch out for include *more/than, but not,* and *as well as.*

Comparisons with these words are tricky but not impossible. Just be sure that the elements you're comparing match grammatically. Check out these examples:

Lulu was more *conservative* than *daring* in her choice of clothes for Larry's wedding.

Even so, Larry liked *the way Lulu moved* but not *the way she looked.*

Lulu enjoyed the ceremonial *garter toss* as well as the ritual *bouquet bonfire.*

The italicized words in each sentence pair off nicely. In the first example, *conservative* and *daring* are both descriptions. In the second, *the way Lulu moved* and *the way she looked* are similar constructions (nouns described by adjective clauses, if you absolutely must know). And in the third example, *garter toss* and *bouquet bonfire* are both nouns.

Here's an incorrect comparison and a possible correction:

> **Wrong:** Ella assumed *that she would live in a separate castle* but not *spending every hour with Larry.*

> **Why it's wrong:** The words *but not* join a subject-verb combination and a verb form.

> **Right:** Ella assumed *that she would live in a separate castle* but not *that she would spend every hour with Larry.*

> **Why it's right:** The sentence compares two subject-verb combinations.

TIP

How do you know how many words of the sentence are being joined? In other words, in the preceding sample sentences, how did I figure out how much to italicize? The decision comes from the meaning of the sentence. Forget grammar for a moment and put yourself into reading comprehension mode. Decide what you're comparing based on the ideas in the sentence. Now check the two ideas being compared and go back into grammar mode. Do the ideas match grammatically? If so, you're fine. If not, reword your sentence.

Chapter **6**

Adjectives, Adverbs, and Comparisons

With the right *nouns* (names of persons, places, things, or ideas) and *verbs* (action or being words), you can construct a solid foundation in a sentence. The key to expressing your precise thoughts is to build on that foundation by adding descriptive words.

In this chapter I explain the two basic types of descriptive words in the English language: *adjectives* and *adverbs*. I show you how to identify them in sentences and how to use each properly. I then walk you through the process of creating descriptive comparisons.

Spotting Adjectives

An *adjective* is a descriptive word that modifies the meaning of a noun or a pronoun. An adjective adds information on number, color, type, and other qualities to your sentence. So when the car you're writing about turns into a *new silver sports* car, you're putting adjectives to work.

Describing nouns and pronouns

The most common job for an adjective is describing a noun. Consider the adjectives *poisonous, angry,* and *rubber* in these sentences. Then decide which sentence you'd like to hear as you walk through the jungle.

> There is an *angry, poisonous* snake on your shoulder.

> There is a *rubber* snake on your shoulder.

In these sentences, the descriptive words certainly make a difference. *Angry, poisonous,* and *rubber* all describe *snake,* and these descriptions give you information that you'd really like to have.

Adjectives can also describe *pronouns* (words that substitute for nouns). When they're giving you information about pronouns, adjectives usually appear after the pronoun they're describing:

> There's something *strange* on your shoulder. (The adjective *strange* describes the pronoun *something.*)

WARNING

A common error is to change certain nouns into adjectives. The word *quality,* for example, is a noun meaning *worth, condition,* or *characteristic.* Some people, especially ad writers, use *quality* as an adjective meaning *good* or *luxurious.* Grammatically, you can't buy a *quality television.* You can, however, buy a *high-quality television.*

Working hand in hand with linking verbs

Adjectives may also follow linking verbs, in which case they describe the subject of the sentence. As I explain in Chapter 2, *linking verbs* join two ideas, associating one with the other. They equate the subject with another idea.

Sometimes a linking verb joins an adjective (or a couple of adjectives) and a noun:

> Lulu's favorite dress is *orange* and *purple.* (The adjectives *orange* and *purple* describe the noun *dress.*)

> George's latest jazz composition sounds *awful.* (The adjective *awful* describes the noun *composition.*)

Recognizing articles as adjectives

If you ran a computer program that sorted and counted every word in this book, you'd find that *articles* are the most common words. Articles — *a, an,* and *the* — occupy a branch on the adjective family tree:

> Melanie wants *the* answer right away.

This statement means that Melanie wants something specific. She is stuck on problem 12, and her mother won't let her go out until her homework is finished. She's on the phone demanding *the* answer to number 12.

> Melanie wants *an* answer right away.

In this case, Melanie isn't quite so specific in her demands. She simply has to have a date for the prom. She asked you a week ago, but if you're not going to be her escort, she'll ask someone else. She's lost patience, and she doesn't even care anymore whether you go. She just wants *an* answer.

REMEMBER

A apple? An book? A precedes words that begin with consonant sounds (all the letters except *a, e, i, o,* and *u*). *An* precedes words that begin with the vowel sounds *a, e, i,* and *o.* The letter *u* is a special case. If the word sounds like *you,* choose *a.* If the word sounds like someone kicked you in the stomach — *uh* — choose *an.* Another special case is the letter *h.* If the word starts with a hard *h* sound, as in *horse,* choose *a.* If the word starts with a silent letter *h,* as in *herb,* choose *an.* Here are some examples:

an aardvark (*a* = vowel)

a belly (*b* = consonant)

a UFO *(U sounds like you)*

an unidentified flying object *(u sounds like uh)*

a helmet (hard *h*)

an hour (silent *h*)

REMEMBER

Special note: Sticklers-for-rules say *an historic event.* The rest of us say *a historic event.*

Locating adjectives

TIP

To find adjectives, go to the words they describe — nouns and pronouns. Start with the noun and ask it three questions: How many? Which one? What kind? Consider this sentence:

> George placed three stolen atomic secrets inside his cheese burrito.

You see three nouns: *George, secrets,* and *burrito.* You can't find the answer to the following questions: How many *Georges?* Which *George?* What kind of *George?* Therefore, no adjectives describe *George.*

But try these three questions on *secrets* and *burrito* and you do come up with something: How many *secrets?* Answer: *three. Three* is an adjective. Which *secrets?* What kind of *secrets?* Answer: *stolen* and *atomic. Stolen* and *atomic* are adjectives. The same goes for *burrito:* What kind? Answer: *cheese. Cheese* is an adjective.

You may have noticed that *his* answers one of the questions. (Which *burrito?* Answer: *his burrito.*) *His* is working as an adjective, but *his* is also a pronoun. Normal people don't have to worry about whether *his* is a pronoun or an adjective. Only English teachers care, and they divide into two camps: the adjective camp and the pronoun camp. Needless to say, each group feels superior to the other. (I'm a noncombatant.)

REMEMBER

Keep in mind, however, that adjectives can also roam around a bit. Here's an example:

> George, *sore* and *tired,* pleaded with Lulu to release him from the headlock she had placed on him when he called her "fragile."

Sore and *tired* tell you about *George. Fragile* tells you about *her.* (Well, *fragile* tells you what George thinks of *her.*) These descriptions come after the words they describe.

Hunting for Adverbs

Adjectives aren't the only descriptive words. *Adverbs* — words that modify the meaning of a verb, an adjective, or another adverb — are also descriptive. Check these out:

> The boss *furiously* said no to Phil's request for a raise.

> The boss *never* said no to Phil's request for a raise.

If you're Phil, you care whether the word *furiously* or *never* is in the sentence. *Furiously* and *never* are adverbs. Notice how adverbs add meaning in these sentences:

> Lola *sadly* sang George's latest song. (Perhaps Lola is in a bad mood.)

> Lola sang George's latest song *reluctantly*. (Lola doesn't want to sing.)

> Lola sang *even* George's latest song. (Lola sang everything, and with George's latest, she hit the bottom of the barrel.)

Sprucing up verbs

Adverbs mostly describe verbs, giving more information about an action. Nearly all adverbs answer one of these four questions: How? When? Where? Why? To find the adverb, go to the verb and ask the four questions. Look at this sentence:

> Ella secretly swiped Sandy's slippers yesterday and then happily went home.

You note two verbs: *swiped* and *went*. Take each one separately. *Swiped* how? Answer: *swiped secretly*. *Secretly* is an adverb. *Swiped* when? Answer: *swiped yesterday*. *Yesterday* is an adverb. *Swiped* where? No answer. *Swiped* why? Knowing Ella, I'd say she stole for the fun of it, but you find no answer in the sentence.

Go on to the second verb in the sentence. *Went* how? Answer: *went happily*. *Happily* is an adverb. *Went* when? Answer: *went then*. *Then* is an adverb. *Went* where? Answer: *went home*. *Home* is an adverb. (For more about the use of *home* as an adverb, see the later "Locating adverbs" section.) *Went* why? Probably to drink champagne out of the slippers, but again, you find no answer in the sentence.

Modifying adjectives and other adverbs

Adverbs also describe other descriptive words (that is, adjectives and adverbs), usually making the description more or less intense. Here's an example:

> An extremely unhappy Larry flipped when his trust fund tanked.

How *unhappy?* Answer: *extremely unhappy. Extremely* is an adverb describing the adjective *unhappy.*

REMEMBER

Sometimes the questions you pose to locate adjectives and adverbs are answered by more than one word in a sentence. In the preceding example sentence, if you ask, "Flipped when?" the answer is *when his trust fund tanked.* Don't panic. These longer answers are just different members of the adjective and adverb families.

Now back to work. Here's another example:

> Larry's frog croaked *quite hoarsely.*

This time an adverb is describing another adverb. *Hoarsely* is an adverb because it explains how the frog *croaked. Quite* is an adverb describing the adverb *hoarsely.*

Locating adverbs

Adverbs can be in lots of places in a sentence. To find them, rely on the questions *how, when, where,* and *why,* not the location. Also consider the following guidelines:

TIP

- » **Many adverbs end in -ly.** Strictly is an adverb, and *strict* is an adjective. *Nicely* is an adverb, and *nice* is an adjective. *Generally* is an adverb, and *general* is an adjective. *Lovely* is a . . . gotcha! You were going to say *adverb,* right? Wrong. *Lovely* is an adjective. (That's why I started this paragraph with *many,* not *all.*)

- » **Some adverbs don't end in -ly.** Soon, *now, home, fast,* and many other words that don't end in -ly are adverbs, too.

> **One of the most common adverbs, *not*, doesn't end in *-ly*.** *Not* is an adverb because it reverses the meaning of the verb from positive to negative. Loosely speaking, *not* answers the question *how*. (*How* are you going to the wedding? Oh, you're *not* going!)

WARNING

Keep in mind that a word may be an adverb in one sentence and something else in another sentence. For example:

Gloria went *home* because of that slammed door.

Home is where the heart is.

Home plate is the umpire's favorite spot.

In the first example, *home* tells you where Gloria went, so *home* is an adverb. In the second example, *home* is a place, so *home* is a noun. In the third example, *home* is an adjective, telling you the kind of *plate*.

Sorting through Some Sticky Choices

Sometimes, deciding whether you need an adjective or an adverb — or identifying which one you have in a sentence — isn't so easy. In this section, I introduce two pairs of tricksters: *good/well* and *bad/badly*. I also put you on alert that — just to make things truly confusing — some adjectives and adverbs look exactly the same.

Choosing between "good" and "well"

How are you doing today? Good? Well? Not sure? If you ever wonder whether you're answering that simple question correctly, this section is for you.

Here's the easy one: *Good* is always an adjective.

I am *good*.

This sentence means *I have the qualities of goodness* or *I am in a good mood.* (Or, the sentence is a really bad pickup line.)

Well is usually, but not always, an adverb:

> I play the piano *well*.

In this sentence, *well* is an adverb. It describes how I play. In other words, the adverb *well* describes the verb *play*.

Where does the "not always" part come in? When you're talking about your health, *well* is an adjective.

> I am *well*.

This sentence means *I am not sick*. In this case, *well* describes the subject *I*, which means it's an adjective.

Do you feel "bad" or "badly"?

Bad is a bad word, at least in terms of grammar. Confusing *bad* and *badly* is one of the most common errors. Check out these examples:

> I felt *badly*.

> I felt *bad*.

Remember the *-ly* test that I mention earlier in this chapter? If so, you know that *badly* is an adverb, and *bad* is an adjective. Which one should you use? Well, what are you trying to say?

In the first sentence, you went to the park with your mittens on. The bench had a sign on it: "Wet Paint." The sign looked old, so you decided to check. You put your hand on the bench, but the mittens were in the way. You felt *badly* — that is, not accurately.

In the second sentence, you sat on the bench, messing up the back of your coat with dark green stripes. When you saw the stripes, you felt *bad* — that is, you were sad.

REMEMBER

In everyday speech, you're not likely to express much about *feeling badly*. About 99.99 percent of the time you feel *bad* — unless, of course, you're in a good mood.

Coping with adjectives and adverbs that look the same

Odd words here and there do double duty as both adjectives and adverbs. They look exactly the same, but they take their identity as adjectives or adverbs from the way that they function in the sentence. Look at these examples:

> Upon seeing the stop sign, Abby stopped *short.* (adverb)
>
> Abby didn't notice the sign until the last minute because she is too *short* to see over the steering wheel. (adjective)
>
> Lola's advice is *right:* Abby shouldn't drive. (adjective)
>
> Abby turned *right* after her last-minute stop. (adverb)

Getting Picky about Word Placement

A few words — *even, almost, nearly, only, just,* and others — often end up in the wrong spot. If you don't place these words correctly, your sentence may say something that you didn't intend.

TEST ALERT

Standardized tests often include sentences misusing these adjectives and adverbs. Double-check every sentence with *even, almost, nearly, only,* and *just.*

Placing "even"

Even is a modifier that can land any place in a sentence — and change its meaning. Take a look at this example:

> It's two hours before the grand opening of the school show. Lulu and George have been rehearsing for weeks, and they know all the dances. Suddenly, George's evil twin Lex "accidentally" places his foot in George's path. George is down! His ankle is sprained! What will happen to the show?

>> **Possibility 1:** Lulu shouts, "We can still go on! *Even Lester* knows the dances."

>> **Possibility 2:** Lulu shouts, "We can still go on! Lester *even knows* the dances."

>> **Possibility 3:** Lulu shouts, "We can still go on! Lester knows *even the dances.*"

What's going on here? These three statements look almost the same, but they aren't. Here's what each one means:

>> **Possibility 1:** Lulu surveys the 15 boys gathered around George. She knows that any one of them could step in at a moment's notice. After all, the dances are easy. *Even Lester,* the clumsiest boy in the class, knows the dances.

>> **Possibility 2:** Lulu surveys the 15 boys gathered around George. Most have been busy learning other parts, and there's no time to teach them George's role. Then she spies Lester. With a gasp, she realizes that Lester has been watching George every minute of rehearsal. Lester doesn't have to practice; he doesn't have to learn something new. Lester *even knows* the dances.

>> **Possibility 3:** The whole group looks at Lester almost as soon as George hits the floor. Yes, Lester knows the words; he's been reciting George's lines for weeks now. Yes, Lester can sing; everyone's heard him. But what about the dances? Just then, Lester begins to twirl around the stage. Lulu sighs with relief. Lester knows *even the dances.* The show will go on!

Even describes the words that follow it. To put it another way, *even* begins a comparison:

>> **Possibility 1:** *even* Lester (as well as everyone else)

>> **Possibility 2:** *even* knows (doesn't have to learn)

>> **Possibility 3:** *even* the dances (as well as the songs and words)

Put *even* at the beginning of the comparison implied in the sentence.

Placing "almost" and "nearly"

Almost and *nearly* are tricky descriptions. For example:

> Last night Lulu wrote for *almost* (or *nearly*) an hour and then went rollerblading.

> Last night Lulu *almost* (or *nearly*) wrote for an hour and then went rollerblading.

In the first sentence, Lulu wrote for 55 minutes and then stopped. In the second sentence, Lulu intended to write, but every time she sat down at the computer, she remembered that she hadn't watered the plants, called her best friend Lola, made a sandwich, and so forth. After an hour of wasted time and without one word on the screen, she grabbed her rollerblades and left.

Almost and *nearly* begin the comparison. Lulu *almost wrote* (or *nearly wrote*), but she didn't. Or Lulu wrote for *almost an hour* (or *nearly an hour*), but not for a *whole hour*. In deciding where to put these words, add the missing ideas and see whether the position of the word makes sense.

Placing "only" and "just"

If only the word *only* were simpler to understand! If everyone thought about the word *just* for *just* a minute. Like the other tricky words in this section, *only* and *just* change the meaning of the sentence every time you alter their positions. Here are examples of *only* and *just* in action:

> *Only* (or *just*) Lex went to Iceland. (No one else went.)

> Lex *only* went to Iceland. (He didn't do anything else.)

> Lex *just* went to Iceland. (The ink on his passport is still wet. *Just* may mean *recently*.)

> Lex went *only* (or *just*) to Iceland. (He skipped Antarctica.)

WARNING

Many people place *only* in front of a verb and assume that it applies to another idea in the sentence. I often see T-shirts with slogans like "My dad went to NYC and only bought me a lousy T-shirt." The *only* should be in front of *a lousy T-shirt* because the sentence implies that Dad should have bought more — the Empire State Building, perhaps.

Creating Comparisons

A common way to use adjectives and adverbs is to create comparisons between two or more things. In this section, I show you how to do so.

Getting the hang of regular comparisons

Take a close look at the comparisons in these sentences:

> Roger's smile is *more evil* than Michael's, but Michael's giggle sounds *cuter*.

> Eggworthy searched for the *least efficient* sports utility vehicle, believing that global warming is *less important* than having the *raciest* image in town.

> Betsy's *most recent* symphony was *less successful* than her *earlier* composition.

What did you notice about the comparisons in the preceding sample sentences? Some of the comparisons are expressed by adding *-er* or *-est*, and some are expressed by adding *more, most, less,* or *least* to the quality that's being compared.

REMEMBER

How do you know which is appropriate? The dictionary is the final authority, and you should consult one if you're in doubt about a particular word. However, here are some general guidelines:

>> You can add *-er* and *-est* to most single-syllable words. (One exception is *fun*. You don't make anything *funner* or *funnest*.)

>> If the word already ends in the letter *e*, you don't double the *e* by adding *-er* or *-est*. Just add *-r* or *-st*.

>> When the descriptive word has more than one syllable, you usually need to use *more, most, less,* and *least* rather than add *-er* or *-est*. I say "usually" because exceptions exist. (If you're *crazy*, you can also be *crazier* and the *craziest*, for example.)

>> *-Er* and *-est* endings aren't usually appropriate for words ending in *-ly*.

Table 6-1 lists some examples of how to add -er and -est to descriptive words to make comparison words.

TABLE 6-1 ## Comparison Forms Using -er and -est

Description of Lola	-er Form	-est Form
able	abler than Lulu	ablest of all the budding scientists
bald	balder than an eagle	baldest of the models
dumb	dumber than a sea slug	dumbest of the congressional candidates
edgy	edgier than caffeine	edgiest of the atom splitters
friendly	friendlier than a grizzly bear	friendliest person on the block
glad	gladder than the loser	gladdest of all the lottery winners

TIP

When the last letter in the descriptive word is y, you must often change the y to i before you tack on the ending.

Table 6-2 contains even more descriptions of Lola, this time with more, less, most, and least added.

TABLE 6-2 ## Two-Word Comparison Forms

Description of Lola	More/Less Form	Most/Least Form
(Lola runs) jerkily	more jerkily than the old horse	most jerkily of all the racers
knock-kneed	less knock-kneed than an old sailor	least knock-kneed of all the beauty pageant contestants
magnificent	more magnificent than a work of art	most magnificent of all the ninjas
rigid	less rigid than a grammarian	least rigid of the traffic cops

These two tables give you a clue about another important comparison characteristic. Did you notice that the second column is always a comparison between Lola and *one other* person or thing? The addition of *-er* or *more* or *less* compares two things. In the last column of each table, Lola is compared to a group with more than two members. When the group is larger than two, *-est* or *most* or *least* creates the comparison and identifies the extreme.

To sum up the rules:

>> Use *-er* or *more/less* when comparing only two things.

>> Use *-est* or *most/least* when singling out the extreme in a group that's larger than two.

>> Never combine two comparison methods, such as *-er* and *more*.

Good, better, best: Working with irregular comparisons

Whenever English grammar gives you a set of rules that make sense, you know the irregulars can't be far behind. Not surprisingly, then, you have to create a few common comparisons without *-er*, *-est*, *more/less*, or *most/least*.

Good, bad, well

I think of these examples as the "report card" comparisons because they evaluate quality. The first word in each of the following bullets provides a description. The second word shows you that description when two elements are being compared. The last word is for comparisons of three or more.

>> Good, better, best

>> Bad, worse, worst

>> Well, better, best

Time to visit *good*, *bad*, and *well* when they're on the job:

> Although Michael's trumpet solo is *good* and Roger's is *better*, Lulu's is the *best* of all.

Lulu's habit of picking at her tattoo is *bad,* but Ralph's constant sneezing is *worse.* Eggworthy's tendency to crack jokes is the *worst* habit of all.

Lola sings *well* in the shower, but Max sings *better* in the bathtub. Ralph croons *best* in the hot tub.

Little, many, much

These are the measuring comparisons — words that tell you about quantity. The first word in each of the following bullets is the description, the second is used for comparisons between two elements, and the last word applies to comparisons of three-plus elements.

- Little, less, least
- Many, more, most
- Much, more, most

Check out these words in action:

Lulu likes a *little* grape jelly on her pizza, but Eggworthy prefers *less* exotic toppings. Of all his creations, Lulu likes chocolate pizza *least.*

Roger spies on *many* occasions, but he seldom uncovers *more* secrets than his brother Al. Lola is the *most* successful spy of all.

Anna has *much* interest in mathematics, though she's *more* devoted to her trumpet lessons. Of all the musical mathematicians I know, Anna is the *most* likely to succeed in both careers.

TIP

Many or *much?* How do you decide which word to use? Easy. *Many* precedes plurals of countable elements (*many crickets* or *many shoes,* for example). *Much* precedes words that express qualities that may not be counted, though these qualities may sometimes be measured (*much noise* or *much sugar,* for instance).

Error alert: Using words that you can't compare

WARNING

Is this chapter more unique than the previous chapter? No, definitely not. Why? Because nothing is *more unique*. The word *unique* means "one of a kind." Either something is one of a kind or it's not. You can't compare something that's unique to anything but itself.

> **Wrong:** The vase that Eggworthy cracked was *more unique* than the Grecian urn.

> **Also wrong:** The vase that Eggworthy cracked was *fairly unique*.

> **Wrong again:** The vase that Eggworthy cracked was *very unique*.

> **Right:** The vase that Eggworthy cracked was *unique*.

REMEMBER

The word *unique* is not unique. Several other words share its absolute quality. One is *perfect*. Something is perfect or not perfect; nothing is *very perfect* or *somewhat perfect*. (I am bound, as a patriotic American, to point out one exception: The U.S. Constitution contains a statement of purpose citing the need to create "a more perfect union.") Another absolute word is *round*. Your shape is *round* or *not round*. Your shape isn't *a bit round*, *rounder*, or *roundest*.

Keep in mind that you *can* use certain adverbs with *unique*, *perfect*, *round*, and the like. For example, you can say something is *nearly perfect* or *almost round*. That's because you can approach an absolute quality, comparing how close someone or something comes to the quality.

WARNING

One more word causes all sorts of trouble in comparisons: *equally*. You hear the expression *equally as* quite frequently. You don't need the *as* because the word *equally* contains the idea of comparison. For example:

> **Wrong:** Roger got a lighter sentence than Lulu, but he is *equally as* guilty.

> **Right:** Roger got a lighter sentence than Lulu, but he is *equally* guilty.

Confusing your reader with incomplete comparisons

What's wrong with this sentence?

> Octavia screamed more chillingly.

The comparison is incomplete. Octavia screamed more chillingly than what? Your readers are left with as many possibilities as they can imagine.

> **Wrong:** Octavia screamed more chillingly.

> **Right:** Octavia screamed more chillingly than I did the day Lulu drove a truck over my toe.

> **Also right:** Octavia screamed more chillingly than she ever had before.

Here's another comparison with a fatal error. Can you spot the problem?

> Lulu loved sky diving more than Lola.

Need a hint? Consider these possible interpretations:

> Lulu loved sky diving more than Lola. Lola sobbed as she realized that Lulu, whom she had always considered her best friend, was on the way to the airport instead of on the way to Lola's party.

or

> Lulu loved sky diving more than Lola. Lola was fine for the first 409 jumps, but then her enthusiasm began to flag. Lulu, on the other hand, was climbing into the airplane eagerly, as if it were her first jump of the day.

See the problem? *Lulu loved sky diving more than Lola* is incomplete. Your reader can understand the comparison in two different ways. The rule here is simple: Don't omit words that are necessary to the meaning of the comparison.

Wrong: Lulu loved sky diving more than Lola.

Right: Lulu loved sky diving more than she loved Lola.

Also right: Lulu loved sky diving more than Lola did.

REMEMBER

Are you *so* tired of comparisons *that* you're ready to send this chapter to the shredder? Well, hang on a little longer as I explain the word *so*. Technically, *so* should be part of a pair — a comparison created with *so* and *that*. Lots of people use *so* alone as an expression of intensity:

Lulu's last sky-dive was *so* spectacular.

The preceding sentence is fine in conversational English. In formal English, however, *so* shouldn't be alone. Finish the comparison, as in this sentence:

Lulu's last sky-dive was *so* spectacular *that* the pilot begged her to fly away with him.

Chapter **7**

Polishing Your Punctuation

If you like rules, this chapter is for you. Whether they're logical or not, you have to follow the punctuation rules I spell out here when you're writing in formal English. Please don't try to memorize them all at once; I don't want to be responsible for the cerebral damage that could result. Instead, use this chapter as a reference when you just can't recall where to put a question mark in a sentence with a quotation or whether a hyphen is necessary in a compound word.

Note: If you're looking for the lowdown on using periods and semicolons, I cover those punctuation marks in Chapter 4, where I talk about constructing sentences.

More Rules Than the IRS: Using Apostrophes

For some reason, even educated people throw apostrophes where they don't belong and leave them out where they're needed. But from now on, you can rise above their ranks. That's because in this section, I explain how to use apostrophes to show ownership and to combine words.

Showing possession

To show possession in French, you say:

the pen of my aunt *(la plume du ma tante)*

You can say the same thing in English, but English also offers another option: the apostrophe. You can keep the same meaning but shorten your phrase this way:

my *aunt's* pen

In this section, I detail how to follow the apostrophe rules when showing possession.

Indicating ownership with singular nouns

When apostrophes show ownership with singular nouns, you add an apostrophe and the letter *s* to the owner:

Michael's gold-filled tooth (The gold-filled tooth belongs to Michael.)

Another way to think about this rule is to see whether the word *of* expresses what you're trying to say. With the *of* method, you note that

the sharp tooth *of* the crocodile = the *crocodile's* sharp tooth

Sometimes, no clear owner appears in a phrase. Such a situation arises mostly when you're talking about time. If you can insert *of* into the sentence, you may need an apostrophe:

a year *of* dental care = a year's dental care

Creating plural possessives

The plurals of most English nouns already end with the letter s. To show ownership, add an apostrophe after the s:

> many *dinosaurs'* petrified teeth (The petrified teeth belong to a herd of dinosaurs.)

TIP

The *of* test works for plurals, too. If you can rephrase the expression using the word *of*, you may need an apostrophe:

> three days *of* dental work = three *days'* dental work

WARNING

Remember that an apostrophe shows ownership. Don't use an apostrophe when you have a plural that is *not* expressing ownership:

Wrong: Bagel's stick to your teeth.

Right: Bagels stick to your teeth.

IRREGULAR PLURAL POSSESSIVES

To show ownership for an *irregular plural* — a plural that doesn't end in s — add an apostrophe and then the letter s. Check out these examples:

> the *children's* erupting teeth (The erupting teeth belong to the children.)

> the *women's* lipstick-stained teeth (The lipstick- stained teeth belong to the women.)

COMPOUND PLURAL POSSESSIVES

What happens when two single people own something? You add one or two apostrophes, depending on the type of ownership. If two people own something together, as a couple, use only one apostrophe:

> George and Martha *Washington's* home (The home belongs to the two of them.)

If two people own things separately, as individuals, use two apostrophes:

> *George's* and *Martha's* teeth (He has his set of teeth, and she has hers.)

Using apostrophes with proper nouns

Companies, stores, and organizations also own things, so these proper nouns — singular or plural — also require apostrophes. Put the apostrophe at the end of the name:

> *Microsoft's* finest operating system
>
> McGillicuddy, Pinch, and *Cinch's* finest lawsuit

Some stores have apostrophes in their names, even without a sense of possession:

> *Macy's* occupies an entire city block.

Macy's is always written with an apostrophe, even when there's no noun after the store name. *Macy's* implies a shortened version of a longer name (perhaps *Macy's Department Store*).

Dealing with compound (hyphenated) words

Other special cases of possession involve compound words: son–in–law, mother–of–pearl, and other words with hyphens. The rule is simple: Put the apostrophe at the end of the word. Never put an apostrophe inside a word. Here are some examples of singular compound nouns:

> the *secretary-treasurer's* report
>
> my *mother-in-law's* teeth

The same rule applies if the hyphenated noun is plural:

> the *doctors-of-philosophy's* study lounge (The study lounge is owned by all the doctors-of-philosophy.)

Tackling possessive nouns that end in s

Singular nouns that end in *s* present special problems. My last name is Woods. My name is singular, because I am only one person. When students talk about me, they may say,

> *Ms. Woods's* grammar lessons can't be beat.

or

> *Ms. Woods'* grammar lessons can't be beat.

REMEMBER

Both (very astute) statements are correct. The Grammar Police have given in on this one because while the first version follows the rules, the second version simply sounds better. Both versions are acceptable, so take your pick.

Showing possession with pronouns

English supplies *pronouns* — words that take the place of a noun — for ownership. Some possessive pronouns are *my, your, his, her, its, our,* and *their.*

REMEMBER

Here's a crucial rule to remember: No possessive pronoun ever has an apostrophe. Here are two examples of possessive pronouns in action:

> that book is *yours*

> *his* call to the police

Cutting it short: Contractions

A *contraction* shortens a word by removing one or more letters and substituting an apostrophe in the same spot. For example, chop *wi* out of *I will*, throw in an apostrophe, and you have *I'll*. The resulting word is shorter and faster to say.

Table 7-1 shows a list of common contractions, including some irregulars. (*Won't*, for example, is short for *will not*.)

If you'd like to make a contraction that isn't in Table 7-1, check your dictionary to make sure it's legal!

TABLE 7-1 **Contractions**

Phrase	Contraction	Phrase	Contraction
are not	aren't	she would	she'd
cannot	can't	that is	that's
could not	couldn't	they are	they're
did not	didn't	they will	they'll
do not	don't	they would	they'd
does not	doesn't	we are	we're
he is	he's	we have	we've
he will	he'll	we will	we'll
he would	he'd	we would	we'd
I am	I'm	what is	what's
I have	I've	who is	who's
I will	I'll	will not	won't
I would	I'd	would not	wouldn't
is not	isn't	you are	you're
it is	it's	you have	you've
she is	she's	you will	you'll
she will	she'll	you would	you'd

Quoting Correctly

A *quotation* is a written repetition of someone else's words — just one word or a whole statement or passage. Quotations pop up in almost all writing. In this section, I show you how to properly punctuate quotations, how to show your reader when the speaker changes, and when to use quotation marks around titles.

Punctuating your quotations

In general, the rules for quotations are simply customs: Put a period inside, put a period outside — what difference does it make to your reader? Not much. But to write proper English, you need to follow all the rules.

Quotations with speaker tags

A *speaker tag* identifies the person(s) being quoted. When the speaker tag comes first, put a comma after it. The period at the end of the sentence goes *inside* the quotation marks.

> The gang remarked, "Lola's candidate is a sure bet."

When the speaker tag comes last, put a comma *inside* the quotation marks and a period at the end of the sentence.

> "I support a different candidate," screamed Lola.

Interrupted quotations

Sometimes a speaker tag lands in the middle of a sentence:

> "I think I'll sue," Betsy explained, "for emotional distress."

Notice all the rules that come into play with an interrupted quotation: The comma is *inside* the quotation marks for the first half of the quotation, and the speaker tag is followed by a comma *before* the quotation marks. The second half of the quotation does not begin with a capital letter, and the period at the end of the sentence is *inside* the quotation marks.

WARNING

When you plop a speaker tag in the middle of someone's conversation, make sure that you don't create a run-on sentence (see Chapter 4). Check out this set of examples:

> **Wrong:** "When you move a piano, you must be careful," squeaked Al, "I could have been killed."

> **Right:** "When you move a piano, you must be careful," squeaked Al. "I could have been killed."

The quoted material forms two complete sentences:

> **Sentence 1:** When you move a piano, you must be careful.

> **Sentence 2:** I could have been killed.

Quoted material doesn't need to express a complete thought, so you don't have to worry about having fragments in your quotations.

Quotations without speaker tags

Not all sentences with quotations include speaker tags. The punctuation and capitalization rules for these sentences are a little different. Check out this example:

> When Michael said that the book "wasn't as exciting as watching paint dry," Anna threw a pie in his face.

If the quotation doesn't have a speaker tag, don't capitalize the first word of the quotation. Also, you don't need a comma to separate the quotation from the rest of the sentence.

Quotations without speaker tags tend to be short — a few words rather than an entire statement. If you're reporting a lengthy statement, you're probably better off with a speaker tag and the complete quotation.

Quotations with question marks

Take a look at these two examples:

> "How can you eat a tuna sandwich while hoisting a piano?" Betsy asked as she eyed his lunch.

> "May I have a bite?" she queried.

The quoted words are questions. If you quote a question, put the question mark *inside* the quotation marks.

Consider a slightly different example: The piano mover answers Betsy, but no one can understand his words. (His mouth is full of tuna fish.) I wonder what he said.

> Did he say, "I can't give you a bite of my sandwich because I ate it all"?

> Did he really declare, "It was just a piano"?

The quoted words in this set are not questions. However, each entire sentence is a question. In this situation, the question mark goes *outside* the quotation marks.

For those rare occasions when both the quoted words and the sentence are questions, put the question mark *inside* the quotation marks:

Did the mover really ask, "Is that lady for real?"

Quotations with exclamation points

Exclamation points follow the same rules as question marks. In other words, if the entire sentence is an exclamation but the quoted words aren't, put the exclamation point *outside* the quotation marks. If the quoted words are an exclamation, put the exclamation point *inside* the quotation marks. If both the sentence and the quotation are exclamations, put the exclamation point *inside* the quotation marks.

Quotations with semicolons

Every hundred years or so you may write a sentence that has both a quotation and a semicolon. (In Chapter 4, I explain semicolons.) When you do, put the semicolon *outside* the quotation marks. Sneak a peek at this example:

Cedric said, "I can't imagine eating anything but vending machine snacks"; his love of junk food was legendary.

Quotations inside quotations

Sometimes you need to place a quotation inside a quotation. A quotation inside another quotation gets single quotation marks. Consider this example:

Archie said, "Al had the nerve to tell me, 'Your pocket protector is nerd-city and dumpster-ready.'"

Without any punctuation, here's what Al said:

Your pocket protector is nerd-city and dumpster-ready.

Without any punctuation, here are all the words that Archie said:

Al had the nerve to tell me your pocket protector is nerd-city and dumpster-ready.

Al's words are a quotation inside another quotation. So you enclose Al's words in single-quotation marks, and you enclose Archie's in double quotation marks.

REMEMBER

Commas and periods follow the same rules in both double and single quotations.

Identifying speaker changes

In a conversation, people take turns speaking:

"You sat on my tuna fish sandwich," Michael said.

"No, I didn't," Ella said.

"Did too," Michael said.

"Did not!" Ella said.

Notice that every time the speaker changes, you form a new paragraph. This way, the conversation is easy to follow because the reader always knows who's talking. Here's another version of the tuna fight:

"You sat on my tuna fish sandwich," Michael said.

"No, I didn't," Ella said.

"Did too."

"Did not!"

Although the speaker tags are left out after the first exchange, you know who's speaking because of the paragraph breaks.

Using quotation marks in titles

In your writing, sometimes you may need to include the title of a magazine, the headline of a newspaper article, and so on. When punctuating these titles, keep in mind these two rules:

REMEMBER

>> For smaller works or parts of a whole, put the title in quotation marks.

>> For larger (complete) works, set the title off from the rest of the writing with italics or underlining.

Use quotation marks for the titles of poems, stories, essays, songs, chapters, magazine or newspaper articles, individual episodes of a TV series, or Web site pages.

Use italics or underlining for the titles of collections of poetry, stories, or essays; books, CDs, magazines, newspapers, TV and radio shows, plays, and entire Web sites.

Here are some examples:

>> "A Thousand Excuses for Missing the Tax Deadline" (a newspaper article) in *The Ticker Tape Journal* (a newspaper)

>> "I Got the W2 Blues" (a song title) on *Me and My Taxes* (a CD containing many songs)

>> "On the Art of Deductions" (an essay) in *Getting Rich and Staying Rich* (a magazine)

>> "Deductions Unlimited" (a page on a Web site) in *Beat the IRS* (the title of a Web site)

WARNING

When a title is alone on a line — on a title page or simply at the top of page one of a paper — don't use italics, quotation marks, or underlining. The centering calls attention to the title. One exception: If part of the title is the name of another work, treat that part as you would any other title. For example, if your brilliant essay is about the magazine *Happy Thoughts*, the title page includes this line:

The Decline of the School Magazine: A Case Study of *Happy Thoughts*

Making Comma Sense

Commas are the sounds of silence — short pauses that provide signals for your reader. Stop here, they say, but not for too long. In this section, I guide you through the rules concerning commas so you know where to put them.

Placing commas in a series

Imagine that you text a shopping list to your roommate Charlie, who's shopping for your birthday party. Everything's on one line.

> butter cookies ice cream cake

How many things does Charlie have to buy? Perhaps two:

>> Butter cookies

>> Ice cream cake

Or perhaps five:

>> Butter

>> Cookies

>> Ice

>> Cream

>> Cake

How does Charlie know? He doesn't, unless you use commas. Charlie actually needs to buy three things: butter cookies, ice cream, and cake. The commas between the items are signals.

REMEMBER

You need commas between each item on the list, with one exception. The comma in front of the word *and* is usually optional. Why? Because when you say *and*, you've already separated the last two items. However, if one of the items in your series includes an *and*, keep the final comma in the series. Here's what I mean:

> For breakfast I ate cereal, ham and eggs, and fruit.

Without the comma after *eggs*, your reader could get confused.

Adding information to your sentence

Your writing relies on nouns and verbs to get your point across. But you also enrich your sentences with descriptions. In this section I explain how to place commas so that your writing expresses what you mean.

Separating descriptions

Writers often string together a bunch of single-word descriptions called *adjectives* (see Chapter 6). If you have a set of descriptions, you probably have a set of commas also. Take a look at the following sentences:

"What do you think of me?" Belle asked Jill.

Jill took a deep breath and said, "I think you're a sniffling, smelly, pimple-tongued, frizzy-haired monster."

Notice the commas in Jill's answer. Four descriptions are listed: *sniffling, smelly, pimple-tongued,* and *frizzy-haired.* A comma separates each description from the next, but there's no comma between the last description (*frizzy-haired*) and the word that it's describing (*monster*).

REMEMBER

Don't separate numbers from other descriptions or from the word(s) they describe, and don't put a comma after a number. Also, don't use commas to separate other descriptions from words that indicate number or amount, such as *many, more, few,* and *less.* More descriptive words that you shouldn't separate from other descriptions or from the words they describe include *other, another, this, that, these,* and *those.* Examine these correctly punctuated sentences:

Sixteen smelly, stained hats were lined up on the shelf.

Many stinky, mud-splattered shoes sat on the floor.

This green, glossy lipstick belongs in her purse.

In your writing, you may create other sentences in which the descriptions shouldn't be separated by commas. For example, sometimes a few descriptive words seem to blend into each other to create one larger description in which one word is clearly more important than the rest. The list of descriptions may provide two or three separate facts about the word that you're describing, but the facts don't deserve equal attention. Look at this example:

Jill just bought that funny little French hat.

You already know that you shouldn't separate *that* from *funny* with a comma. But what about *funny, little,* and *French*? If you write

> Jill just bought that funny, little, French hat.

you're giving equal weight to each of the three descriptions. Do you really want to emphasize all three qualities? Probably not. In fact, you're probably not making a big deal out of the fact that the hat is *funny* and *little.* Instead, you're emphasizing that the hat is *French.* So you don't need to put commas between the other descriptions.

TIP

Sentences like this example require judgment calls. Use this rule as a guide: If the items in a description aren't of equal importance, don't separate them with commas.

Distinguishing essential information from extras

Sometimes your descriptions are longer than one word. If a description is essential to the meaning of the sentence, don't put commas around it. If the description provides extra, nonessential information, set it off with commas.

TEST ALERT

If you expect to darken little ovals with a #2 pencil, spend a little extra time in this section and the next, "Commas with appositive influence." Both the SAT and the ACT gauge your knowledge of essential and nonessential commas.

Consider an example. In her quest to reform Larry's government, Ella made this statement:

> Taxes, which are a hardship for the people, are not acceptable.

Lou, who is a member of Larry's Parliament, issued the same statement but with no commas:

> Taxes which are a hardship for the people are not acceptable.

Do the commas really matter? Yes. They matter a lot. Here's the deal: If the description *which are a hardship for the people* is set off from the rest of the sentence by commas, the description is extra — not essential to the meaning of the sentence. You can cross it out and the sentence still means the same thing. If commas don't set off the description, however, the description is essential to the meaning of the sentence. Can you see the difference between Ella's statement and Lou's? Here's a revised version of each statement:

Ella: The government should not impose taxes.

Lou: The government is against any taxes that are a hardship for the people.

Lou's proposal is much less extreme than Ella's. Lou opposes only some taxes — those he believes are a burden.

The pronouns *which* and *that* may help you decide whether you need commas. *That* generally introduces information that the sentence can't do without — essential information that you don't set off with commas. The pronoun *which* often introduces nonessential information that may be surrounded by commas. However, these distinctions aren't always true.

At the beginning of a sentence, a phrase that starts with "because" acts as an introductory remark and is always set off by a comma:

Because the tattoo was on sale, Lulu whipped out her credit card and rolled up her sleeve.

At the end of a sentence, the "because" statement is sometimes set off by commas, in which case it may be lifted out of the sentence without changing the meaning. Without commas, it's essential to the meaning. Take a look at these two statements:

With commas: Lulu didn't get that tattoo, because it was in bad taste.

Meaning: No tattoos for Lulu! The "because" information is extra, explaining why Lulu passed on the design.

Without commas: Lulu didn't get that tattoo because it was in bad taste.

Meaning: Lulu got the tattoo, but not because it was in bad taste. She got it for another reason (perhaps the sale).

Commas with appositive influence

If you're seeing double when you read a sentence, you've probably encountered an *appositive*. Strictly speaking, appositives aren't descriptions, though they do give you information about something else in the sentence. Appositives are nouns or pronouns that are exactly the same as the noun or pronoun preceding them in the sentence. You set off some appositives with commas, and others you don't.

REMEMBER

Here's the rule concerning commas and appositives: If you're sure that your readers will know what you're talking about before they get to the appositive, set off the appositive with commas. If you're not sure your readers will know exactly what you're talking about by the time they arrive at the appositive, you shouldn't use commas.

Here's an example in which *Mary* is the appositive of *sister*:

> Lulu has five sisters, but her sister Mary is definitely her favorite.

Because Lulu has five sisters, you don't know which sister is being discussed until you have the name. *Mary* identifies the sister and shouldn't be placed between commas. Here's another example:

> Roger has only one sibling. His sister, Mary, doesn't approve of Roger's espionage.

Because Roger has only one sibling, the reader knows that he has only one sister. Thus the words *his sister* pinpoint the person being discussed in the sentence. The name is extra information, so you should set it off with commas.

Directly addressing someone

When writing a message to someone, you need to separate the person's name from the rest of the sentence with a comma. Otherwise, your reader may misread the message. Look at two versions of a note that Michael left on a door:

> Roger wants to kill Wendy. I locked him in this room.

> Roger wants to kill, Wendy. I locked him in this room.

In the first sentence, Roger wants to kill one specific person; only Wendy needs to run for her life. In the second sentence, everyone is in danger. The note is intended for Wendy, but Roger doesn't seem to care whom he kills.

In grammarspeak, the second version is a *direct-address* sentence. The writer is directing his comments to Wendy, so her name is cut off from the rest of the sentence with a comma. Direct address is also possible at the beginning or in the middle of a sentence:

> Wendy, Roger wants to kill, so I locked him in this room.

> Roger wants to kill, Wendy, so I locked him in this room.

Presenting addresses and dates

Commas are good, all-purpose separators, and they do a fine job on addresses and dates.

Addressing addresses

Here's an address, the way you see it on an envelope:

> Ms. Belle Planet
>
> 223 Center Street
>
> Venus, New York 10001

If you put Belle's address into a sentence, you have to separate each item of the address:

> Belle Planet lives at 223 Center Street, Venus, New York 10001.

Notice that the house number and street aren't separated by a comma, nor are the state and zip code.

If the sentence continues, you must separate the last item in the address from the rest of the sentence with another comma:

> Belle Planet lives at 223 Center Street, Venus, New York 10001, but is thinking of moving to Mars.

If you have just a city and a state, put a comma between them. If the sentence continues, place a comma after the state.

> Belle Planet lives in Venus, New York, but is thinking of moving to Mars.

Punctuating dates

Confession time: The rules for placing commas in dates aren't very stable these days. Also, writers from different areas (science and literature, for example) favor different systems. In this section I tell you the traditional form and show you some possible variations. If you're writing for business or school, the traditional form should get you through.

If the date is alone on a line (perhaps at the top of a letter), these formats are fine:

September 28, 2060 (traditional)

28, 2060 (traditional)

28 September 2060 (modern in the United States, traditional in many other countries)

When dates appear in a sentence, the format changes depending on (a) how traditional you want to be and (b) how much information you want to give. Take a look at the commas — or the lack of commas — in these sentences:

On September 28, 2060, Lulu ate several thousand gummy candies. (traditional)

In October, 2060, Lulu gave up sugary snacks. (traditional)

Lulu pigs out every October 31st. (both camps)

In October 2060 Lulu suffered from severe indigestion. (modern)

Lulu visited a nutritionist on 20 October 2060. (modern)

Setting off introductory words

Yes, this section introduces a comma rule. Well, you probably know it already. Oh, I'll explain it anyway. Okay, the rule is that you must separate words that aren't part of the sentence but instead comment on the meaning of the sentence. In other words, you use commas to set off *introductory words* at the beginning of a sentence from what follows. If you omit these words, the sentence still means the same thing. Common examples include *yes, no, well, oh,* and *okay.*

Read these examples twice, once with the introductory words and once without. See how the meaning stays the same?

> Yes, you are allowed to chew gumballs during class.

> Well, you may consider moving on to another topic if you have exhausted "My Favorite Lightbulb."

Punctuating with conjunctions

When you join two complete sentences with the conjunctions (joining words) *and, or, but, nor, yet, so,* or *for,* place a comma before the conjunction. Some examples:

> Agnes robbed the bank, and then she went out for a hamburger.

> James spies, but apart from that lapse he is not a bad fellow.

For more information on conjunctions and complete sentences, see Chapter 4.

WARNING

Some sentences have one subject and two verbs joined by *and, but, or,* or *nor.* Don't put commas between the two verbs. You aren't joining two complete sentences, just two words or groups of words. Here's an example:

> **Wrong:** Ella wrote a statement for the media, and then screamed at her press agent for an hour.

> **Why it's wrong:** The sentence has one subject *(Ella)* and two verbs *(wrote, screamed).* You aren't joining two complete sentences, so you shouldn't place a comma before *and.*

> **Right:** Ella wrote a statement for the media and then screamed at her press agent for an hour.

Mastering Dashes

Long dashes — what grammarians call *em dashes* — are dramatic. These long straight lines draw your eye and hold your attention. But long dashes aren't just showoffs; they insert information into a sentence and introduce lists. Short dashes — *en dashes* — show a range or connect words when the word *to* or *and* is implied.

Long dashes

A long dash's primary job is to tell the reader that you've jumped tracks onto a new (though related) subject, just for a moment. Here's an example:

> After we buy toenail clippers — the dinosaur in that exhibit could use a trim — we'll go to the bakery.

The information inside the dashes is off-topic. Take it out, and the sentence makes sense. The material inside the dashes relates to the information in the rest of the sentence, but it acts as an interruption to the main point that you're making.

TEST ALERT

The words between a pair of dashes may or may not form a complete sentence. Fine. However, some people use only one dash to tack a complete sentence onto another complete sentence. Not fine! (This is an issue you may encounter on standardized tests.) Here's what I mean:

> **Wrong:** The curator painted the dinosaur orange — everyone hates the color.

> **Right:** The curator painted the dinosaur orange — everyone hates the color — because she wanted to "liven the place up."

> **Also right:** The curator painted the dinosaur orange; everyone hates the color.

The first example sentence is wrong because a dash can't link two complete sentences. The second example is okay because a pair of dashes can surround a complete sentence embedded inside another complete sentence. The third example avoids the problem by linking the two sentences with a semicolon.

Short dashes

If you master this punctuation mark, you deserve an official grammarian's badge. Short dashes show a range:

> From May–September, the convicts prune commas from literature written over the winter.

Short dashes also show up when you're omitting the word *to* between two elements:

> The New York–Philly train is always on time.

Finally, a short dash links two or more equal elements when *and* is implied:

> The catcher–pitcher relationship is crucial.

Don't confuse short dashes with hyphens, an even shorter punctuation mark that I cover in the next section.

Wielding Hyphens with Ease

You need hyphens to separate parts of compound words, to write certain numbers, and to create one description from two words. This section provides you with a guide to the care and feeding of the humble hyphen.

Creating compound words

Hyphens separate parts of compound words, such as *ex-wife, pro-choice, mother-in-law*, and so forth. When you write these words, don't put a space before or after the hyphen.

The trend these days is toward using fewer punctuation marks. Thus, many words that used to be hyphenated compounds are now written as single words. *Semi-colon*, for instance, has morphed into *semicolon*. The dictionary is your friend when you're figuring out whether an expression is a compound, a single word, or two separate words.

Hyphens also show up when a single word could be misunderstood. I once received an e-mail from a student. "I resent the draft," she wrote. I spent ten minutes worrying about her feelings before I realized that she sent the draft twice because the e-mail didn't go through the first time. To avoid misinterpretation, she should have written *re-sent*.

Hyphenating numbers

Decisions about whether to write a numeral or a word are questions of style, not of grammar. The authority figure in your life — teacher, boss, whatever — will tell you what he or she prefers. In general, you usually represent larger numbers with numerals:

> Roger has been arrested 683 times, counting last night.

However, on various occasions you may need to write the word, not the numeral. If the number falls at the beginning of a sentence, for example, you must use words because no sentence may begin with a numeral. You may also need to write about a fractional amount. Here's how to hyphenate:

REMEMBER

>> Hyphenate all numbers from twenty-one to ninety-nine.

>> Hyphenate all fractions used as descriptions (*three-quarters full,* for example).

>> Don't hyphenate fractions used as nouns (*three quarters of the money; one third of all registered voters*).

Connecting two-word descriptions

If two words create a single description, put a hyphen between them if the description comes before the word that it's describing. For example:

> a *well-placed* hyphen — BUT — the hyphen is *well placed*

WARNING

Don't hyphenate two-word descriptions if the first word ends in -*ly*:

> *nicely drawn* rectangle

> *completely ridiculous* grammar rule

Creating a Stopping Point: Colons

A colon (:) appears when a comma isn't strong enough. In this section I look at the colon in a few of its natural habitats: business letters, lists, and quotations.

Sprucing up a business letter

Colons appear in business letters after the *salutation:* the "Dear Ms. X" or "To Whom It May Concern." The colon makes a business letter more formal. The opposite of a business letter is what English teachers call a *friendly letter* (even if it says something like "I hate you"). When you write a friendly letter, put a comma after the name of the person who will receive it.

Inserting long lists

When you insert a short list of items into a sentence, you don't need a colon. When you insert a long list into a sentence, however, you may use a colon to introduce it. Think of the colon as a gulp of air that readies the reader for a good-sized list. The colon precedes the first item. Here's a sentence that uses a colon to introduce a list:

> General Parker needed quite a few things: a horse, an army, a suit of armor, a few million arrows, and a map.

WARNING

If you put a colon in front of a list, check the part of the sentence before the colon. Can it stand alone? If so, great. The words before the colon must form a complete thought. If not, don't use a colon.

Introducing long quotations

The rule concerning colons with quotations is fairly easy. If the quotation is short, introduce it with a comma. If the quotation is long, introduce it with a colon:

> Lola stated, "I have no comment."

> Parker explained: "The media has been entirely too critical of my preparations for war. Despite the fact that I have spent the last ten years and two million gold coins perfecting new and improved armor, I have been told that I am unready to fight."

REMEMBER

When you write a paper for school, you may put some short quotations (up to three lines) into the text. If a quotation is longer than three lines, you should double-indent and single-space the quoted material so that it looks like a separate block of print. Such quotations are called *block quotations.* Introduce the blocked quotation with a colon, and don't use quotation marks. Here's an example:

Flugle makes the following point about homework:

> Studies show that students who have no time to rest are not as efficient as those who do. When a thousand teens were surveyed, they all indicated that sleeping, listening to music, talking on the phone, and watching TV were more valuable than schoolwork.

Colons sometimes also join one complete sentence to another. You may use a colon this way only when the second sentence explains the meaning of the first sentence, as in this example:

> Lola has refused to take the job: She believes the media will investigate every aspect of her life.

Notice that I capitalize the first word after the colon. Some writers prefer lowercase for that spot. This decision is a matter of style, not grammar. Check with the authority figure in charge of your writing for his or her preference.

Chapter **8**

Capitalizing Correctly

E very teacher has at least one pet peeve. I have a good-sized set of usage errors that set my teeth on edge. One is using lowercase for the personal pronoun *I*. It's not that I have anything against lowercase letters. It's just that I believe *i* and *I* should follow tradition, because, well . . . capitalization is all about tradition. So don't look for logic in this chapter. All you find here is what's up with capitalization rules.

Covering the Basic Rules

Fortunately, the rules for capital letters are easy. Here are the basics:

» **Begin every sentence with a capital letter.** What's that you asked? What about sentences that begin with a numeral? Caught you! You're not supposed to begin a sentence with a numeral. Ever. If you need a number in that spot, you have to write the word and capitalize it. So if you're a star pitcher and the Yankees make an offer, don't send this text:

$10,000,000 per game is not enough.

Instead, type one of these messages:

A mere $10,000,000 per game is not enough.

Ten million dollars per game is not enough.

Traditionally, the first letter of each line of a poem is capitalized, even if it isn't the beginning of a sentence. However, poets enjoy trashing (sorry, I meant *reinterpreting*) rules. In poetry, anything goes — including capitalization rules.

>> **Capitalize *I*.** I have no idea why the personal pronoun *I* must be capitalized, but it must. So save lowercase for other pronouns (*he, she, us, them,* and so on).

>> **Capitalize names.** This rule applies when you're using an actual name, not a category. Write about *Elizabeth,* not *elizabeth,* when you're discussing the cutest baby ever (my granddaughter). She's a *girl,* not a *Girl,* because *girl* is a category, not a name. Elizabeth lives in *Washington,* not *washington* (her *state,* not her *State,* because *state* is a general category, not a name). You also capitalize brand names (*Sony,* for example) unless the company itself uses lowercase letters (the *iPod,* for instance).

TIP

When dealing with company and product names, you often run into unusual capitalization situations. (Think *eBay* and *BlackBerry,* for example.) Your best bet is to go to the company's authorized Web site and see how the name appears there.

>> **Capitalize words that refer to the deity.** Traditionally, believers capitalize all words that refer to the being they worship, as in this line from a famous hymn:

God works in mysterious ways *His* wonders to perform.

Capitalize mythological gods only when giving their names:

The ancient Greeks built temples in honor of *Zeus* and other *gods.*

>> **Begin most quotations with a capital letter.** When quotation marks appear, so do capitals — most of the time. (For exceptions to this rule, turn to Chapter 7.)

That's it for the basics. For the picky stuff, keep reading.

Capitalizing (Or Not) References to People

If human beings were called only by their names, life would be much simpler, at least in terms of capital letters. But most people pick up a few titles and some relatives as they journey through life.

In this section I tell you what to capitalize when you're referring to people.

Treating a person's titles with care

Allow me to introduce myself. I'm *Ms.* Woods, *Chief Grammarian* Woods, and *Apostrophe-Hater-in-Chief* Woods. All these titles start with capital letters because they're attached to the front of my name. In a sense, they've become part of my name.

Allow me to introduce my friend Eggworthy. He's *Mr.* Eggworthy Henhuff, *director of poultry* at a nearby farm. Next year, *Director of Poultry* Henhuff plans to run for *state senator,* unless he cracks under the pressure of a major campaign, in which case he'll run for *sheriff.*

Now what's going on with the capitals? The title *Mr.* is capitalized because it's attached to Eggworthy's last name. Other titles — *state senator* and *sheriff* — are not. In general, lowercase titles are those not connected to a name.

Notice that *Director of Poultry* is capitalized when it precedes Eggworthy's last name but not capitalized when it follows Eggworthy's name. *Director of Poultry Henhuff* functions as a unit. If you were talking to Eggworthy, you might address him as *Director of Poultry Henhuff.* So the first *Director of Poultry* in this paragraph functions as part of the name. When the title follows the name, it gives the reader more information about Eggworthy, but it no longer acts as part of Eggworthy's name. Hence, the second *director of poultry* in the paragraph is in lowercase.

WARNING

No self-respecting rule allows itself to be taken for granted, however. You may need to capitalize very important titles, even when they appear without the name of the people who hold them. What's very important? Definitely these:

>> President of the United States

>> Secretary General of the United Nations

>> Chief Justice of the Supreme Court

>> Prime Minister of Great Britain

The rules on capitalizing these titles differ depending on your audience and the style guide you're following. When in doubt, check with your boss, editor, teacher, or other authority figure about how to treat important titles.

The following titles are often — but not always — lowercase when they appear without a name:

>> ambassador

>> cabinet secretary

>> consul

>> judge

>> mayor

>> representative

Nameless titles that are even lower on the importance ladder are strictly lowercase, such as *assistant secretary, officer,* and *ensign.*

When capitalizing a two-word title, capitalize both words (*Chief Justice*) or neither (*assistant secretary*). One exception (sigh) to the rule is for *exes* and *elects:*

>> ex-President

>> President-elect

Handling family relationships

It's not true that Elizabeth's *grandma* was imprisoned for felonious sentence structure. I know for a fact that *Uncle Bart* took the rap, although his *brother* Alfred tried desperately to persuade *Grandma* to make a full confession. "My *son* deserves to do time," said *Grandma,* "because he split an infinitive when he was little and got away with it."

What do you notice about the family titles in the preceding paragraph? Some of them are capitalized, and some are not. The rules for capitalizing the titles of family members are simple. If you're labeling a relative, don't capitalize. (I'm talking about kinship labels here: *aunt, sister, son,* and so on.) If the titles take the place of names (as in *Uncle Bart* and *Grandma*), capitalize them. For example:

> Lulu's *stepsister* Sarah took care to pour exactly one cup of ink into every load of wash that Lulu did. (*stepsister* = label)

> Sarah told *Mother* about the gallon of paint thinner that Lulu had dripped over Sarah's favorite rose bush. (*Mother* = name)

> I was surprised when my *father* took no action; fortunately, *Aunt Aggie* stepped in with a pail of bleach for Lulu. (*father* = label; *Aunt Aggie* = name)

TIP

If you can substitute a real name for the reference to the person in the sentence, you probably need a capital letter:

> **Original:** I told *Father* that he needed to shave off his handlebar mustache and put it on his bicycle.

> **Substitution:** I told *Jonas* that he needed to shave off his handlebar mustache and put it on his bicycle.

In this case, the substitution sounds fine, so capitalize *Father*.

If the substitution sounds strange, you probably need lowercase:

> **Original:** I told my *grandmother* not to shave off her mustache.

> **Substitution:** I told my *Mabel* not to shave off her mustache.

The substitution doesn't work because you don't say *my Mabel*. In this example, you use lowercase for *grandmother*.

TIP

The word *my* and other possessive pronouns (*your, his, her, our, their*) often indicate that you should lowercase the title. (For more information on possessive pronouns, see Chapter 3.)

Tackling race and ethnicity

If you come from Tasmania, you're Tasmanian. If you come from New York, you're a New Yorker. (Don't ask me about Connecticut; I've never been able to get an answer, though I've asked everyone I know from that state.) Those examples of capitalization are easy. But what about race and ethnicity?

Like everyone else, grammarians struggle to overcome the legacy of a racist society and its language. Here are some guidelines concerning capitalization and race:

>> White and Black (or white and black) are acceptable descriptions, but be consistent. Don't capitalize one and not the other. Always capitalize *Asian* because the term is derived from the name of a continent.

>> European American, Asian American, and African American are all in capitals, as are other descriptions of origin derived from place names, such as Mexican American and Polish American.

Getting a Geography Lesson: Places, Directions, and More

This section covers capitalizing all things geographical: the names of places, languages, geographical features, regions, and directions.

Locations and languages

In general, you should capitalize the names of countries and languages. Of course, exceptions exist. Some common objects with a country or nationality as part of the name may not need to be capitalized; *scotch whisky* and *venetian blinds* are examples. But *Brussels sprouts* and *Yorkshire terrier* do require capitalization. Confusing? You bet. Bottom line: If you're not sure whether to capitalize the geographical part of a common item, check the dictionary.

Capitalize locations within a country — cities or regions, for example — when the proper name is given: the *Mississippi River*, the *Congo*, or *Los Angeles*, for example. Is *the* ever part of the name? Usually not, even when it's hard to imagine the name without it. In general, don't capitalize *the*.

When referring to geographical features instead of proper names, don't capitalize: *mountain, valley, gorge,* or *beach,* for instance.

Directions and areas

Robbie and Levon, my parakeets, don't migrate for the winter. (Instead, they sit on the window frame and squawk at their friends, the pigeons of New York.) If they did fly away, though, where would they go: south or South? It depends. The direction of flight is *south* (lowercase). The area of the country where they work on a tan is the *South* (uppercase). Got it? From New York City you drive *west* to visit the *West* (or the *Midwest*).

You often capitalize the names of other, smaller areas as well. Plopped in the center of New York City is Central Park, which the city's West Side and East Side flank. Chicago has a South Side and London has Bloomsbury. Note the capital letters for the names of these areas.

Looking at Seasons and Times of Day

Loch Ness hates the *summer* because of all the tourists who try to snap pictures of what he calls "an imaginary monster." He has been known to roar something about *"winter's* peaceful *mornings,"* even though he never wakes up before *3 p.m.*

After reading the preceding example, you can probably figure out this rule without me. Write the seasons of the year in lowercase, as well as the times of day.

TIP

Some books tell you to capitalize the abbreviations for morning and afternoon (*A.M.* and *P.M.*) and some specify lowercase (*a.m.* and *p.m.*). So no matter what you do, half your readers will think you're right and half will think you're wrong. Your best bet is to check with the authority overseeing your writing. If you're the authority, do what you want.

Getting Schooled in Education Terms

As every student knows, school is complicated. So is the rule concerning the capitalization of school-related terms. Don't capitalize subjects and subject areas (*history, science,* and *physics,* for example) unless the name refers to a language (*Spanish,*

Latin, English, and so on). On the other hand, capitalize the titles of courses (*Economics 101, Math for Poets, Paper Clips in American History,* and the like).

The years in school, though interminable and incredibly important, are not capitalized (*seventh grader, freshman,* and *sophomore,* for instance).

Wrestling with Capitals in Titles

Loch Ness is hosting a party to celebrate the publication of his new book, *I AM NOT A MONSTER.* He has postponed the party three times because he can't decide how to capitalize the title. What should he do?

>> **Capitalize *I* and *Monster.*** *I* is always uppercase, and *Monster* is an important word. Also, *I* is the first word of the title, and you always capitalize the first word of a title.

>> **Capitalize *Am.*** It's a verb, and verbs are at the heart of the title's meaning.

>> **Capitalize *Not.*** This word changes the meaning of the verb and thus has an important job to do in the sentence.

>> **Lowercase the only word left — *a.*** Never capitalize articles (*a, an,* and *the*) unless they're the first words in the title.

The resulting book title is *I Am Not a Monster.*

Here's a summary of the rules for all sorts of titles:

>> Capitalize the first word in the title.

>> Capitalize verbs and other important words.

>> Lowercase unimportant words: articles *(a, an, the),* conjunctions (words that connect, such as *and, or,* and *nor*), and prepositions (*of, with, by,* and other words that express a relationship between two elements in the sentence).

TIP

Some grammarians capitalize long prepositions — those with more than four letters. Others tell you to lowercase all prepositions, even the huge ones, such as *concerning* and *according to*. (See Chapter 10 for a list of common prepositions.) Your best bet is to check with your immediate authority (editor, boss, teacher, and so on) to make sure that you write in the style to which he or she is accustomed.

WARNING

When writing the title of a magazine or newspaper, should you capitalize the word *the*? Yes, if *the* is part of the official name, as in *The New York Times*. No, if the publication doesn't include *the* in its official name, as in the *Daily News*.

Writing about Events and Eras

Jane entered her time machine and set the dial for the *Middle Ages*. Because of a glitch in the power supply, Jane ended up right in the middle of the *Industrial Revolution*. Fortunately for Jane, the *Industrial Revolution* did not involve a real *war*. Jane still shudders when she remembers her brief stint in the *Civil War*. She is simply not cut out to be a fighter, especially not a fighter in the *nineteenth century*. On the next *Fourth of July*, Jane plans to fly the bullet-ridden flag she brought back from the *Battle of Gettysburg*.

The moral of Jane's story? Capitalize the names of specific time periods and events but not general words. Hence,

» Capitals: Middle Ages, Industrial Revolution, Civil War, Fourth of July, Battle of Gettysburg

» Lowercase: war, nineteenth century

REMEMBER

Some grammarians capitalize *Nineteenth Century* because they see it as a specific time period. Others say that you should lowercase numbered centuries. I prefer to lowercase the century. However, you need to make certain that you're even supposed to spell out *nineteenth* in this situation; your authority figure or style guide may demand *19th* instead.

Capitalizing Abbreviations

I often discourage abbreviations because they can confuse the reader and because they clash with formal writing. Sometimes, however, you do want to abbreviate. Here's how to do so correctly:

>> Capitalize abbreviations for titles, and end the abbreviation with a period. For example, *Mrs.* Snodgrass, *Rev.* Tawkalot, *Sen.* Veto, and Jeremiah Jones, *Jr.*

>> Capitalize geographic abbreviations when they're part of a proper name, and put a period at the end: Appalachian *Mts.* or Amazon *R.,* for example.

>> The United States Postal Service has devised a list of two-letter state abbreviations. Don't put periods in these abbreviations, such as *AZ* (Arizona) and *CO* (Colorado).

>> Write most measurements in lowercase, and end the abbreviation with a period (*yds.* for *yards* or *lbs.* for *pounds*). Metric abbreviations are sometimes written without periods (*km* for *kilometer* or *g* for *gram*).

WARNING

Don't confuse abbreviations with acronyms. Abbreviations generally chop some letters out of a single word. Acronyms are new words made from the first letters of each word in a multiword title, such as these examples:

NATO: North Atlantic Treaty Organization

OPEC: Organization of the Petroleum Exporting Countries

AIDS: Acquired Immune Deficiency Syndrome

WARNING

Want to drive your teacher crazy? Write a formal essay with &, *w/*, *w/o*, or *b/c*. These symbols are fine for your notes but not for your finished product. Similarly, save *brb (be right back), lol (laugh out loud),* and other texting abbreviations for your friends, not for authority figures.

Chapter 9

Choosing the Right Words

This chapter is chock-full of grammar demons that can trip up even the most seasoned writers. None of the rules I explain here are particularly difficult to master; the problem is trying to keep them all in mind when you're writing a 20-page report.

TIP

Here's what I suggest: Try to commit as much of this information to memory as possible, but also keep this chapter handy as a reference. Pull it out when you're proofreading your work, and chances are you'll catch a mistake or two that slipped through. (Better you than your boss or teacher, right?)

One Word or Two?

In this section, I list some common two-word phrases that people like to write (mistakenly) as single words. I also show you some pairs of words that have very different meanings depending on whether they're written as two words or squeezed together into one.

Always opting for two

The following words are often written as one — incorrectly! Always write them as two separate words:

>> **A lot:** This one gets misspelled a lot.

>> **All right:** It's never all right to make this a single word.

>> **Each other:** We can keep each other happy by writing this as two words.

Picking your meaning

You can write the following words as one or two words, but be aware that they have different meanings:

>> **Altogether** means "extremely, entirely."

>> **All together** means "as one."

Example: Daniel was *altogether* disgusted with the way the entire flock of dodo birds sang *all together*.

>> **Sometime** means "at a certain point in time."

>> **Some time** means "a period of time."

Example: Lex said that he would visit Lulu *sometime*, but not now because he has to spend *some time* in jail for murdering the English language.

>> **Someplace** means "an unspecified place" and describes an action.

>> **Some place** means "a place" and refers to a physical space.

Example: Lex screamed, "I have to go *someplace* now!" Lulu thinks he headed for *some place* near the railroad station.

>> **Everyday** means "ordinary, common."

>> **Every day** means "occurring daily."

Example: Larry loves *everyday* activities such as cooking, cleaning, and sewing. He has the palace staff perform all these duties *every day*.

>> **Anyway** means "in any event."

>> **Any way** means "a way" or "some sort of way."

Example: "*Anyway*," added Roy, "I don't think there's *any way* to avoid jail for tax evasion."

>> **Awhile** means (confusingly enough) "for a while."

>> **A while** means "a period of time."

Example: I think I'll wait *awhile* before telling my parents I don't want to get a job for *a while*.

Separating Possessive Pronouns from Contractions

The word pairs in this section sound the same but aren't. Each case has one form that shows possession and another that's a *contraction* (a combination of two words shortened by using an apostrophe). One case (the word *there*) even has a third word that sounds the same as the possessive and contraction forms but bears no relation to them whatsoever in terms of meaning.

REMEMBER

Here are two rules you must commit to memory to avoid mistakes with these word pairs:

>> No possessive pronoun ever has an apostrophe. Ever. (See Chapter 3 for a discussion of possessive pronouns.)

>> A contraction always has an apostrophe. Always. (Chapter 7 gives you the lowdown on contractions.)

Its/it's

This word pair may win the prize for causing the most confusion. I see *it's* mistakenly used to show possession on storefronts, on billboards, and even in newspaper articles. (The horror!)

I understand the source of confusion here: People who use *it's* to show possession are remembering that you add an *'s* whenever you have a singular noun (see Chapter 7). But pronouns are different! As I note at the beginning of this section, no possessive pronoun ever has an apostrophe. Ever.

So here's what you need to know: *Its* shows possession, and *it's* means "it is":

> The computer has exploded, and *its* screen is now decorating the ceiling.

> *It's* raining cats and dogs, but I don't see any alligators.

Your/you're

You're in trouble if your apostrophes are in the wrong place, especially when you're writing in the second person. (The second person is the form that uses *you*, *your*, and *yours*.) *You're* means "you are." *Your* shows possession. These two words are not interchangeable. Some examples:

> *"You're* not going to eat that rotten pumpkin," declared Rachel.

> *"Your* refusal to eat the pumpkin means that you will be given mystery meat instead," commented Dean.

There/their/they're

There is a place. *Their* shows ownership. *They're* is short for "they are." Some examples:

> *"They're* too short," muttered Eggworthy as he eyed the strips of bacon.

> "Why don't you take some longer strips from *their* plates," suggested Lola.

> "My arm is not long enough to reach over *there*," sighed Eggworthy.

Whose/who's

Whose shows ownership. It seldom causes any problems, except when it's confused with another word: who's. *Who's* is a contraction that's short for "who is." For example:

> The boy *whose* hat was burning was last seen running down the street screaming, *"Who's* in charge of fire fighting in this town?"

Using Words That Seem Interchangeable but Aren't

This section features pairs of words that many writers assume mean the same thing. In each case, that assumption is wrong. Sometimes the distinctions may seem trivial, but they're real enough to cause trouble if you make the wrong choice on a standardized test or in your big report to the boss.

Affect versus effect

Has the study of grammar affected or effected your brain? Usually, *affect* is a verb that means "to influence" and *effect* is a noun meaning "result." Here's how they work in a sentence:

> Sunlight *affects* Ludwig's appetite; he never eats during the day.

> Ludmilla thinks that her vegetarian pizza will *affect* Ludwig's dietary regimen, but I think the *effect* will be disastrous.

However, just to keep things utterly confusing, each word has a second usage and meaning:

>> *Affect* may be a noun meaning "the way one relates to and shows emotions." Huh? Honestly, you rarely encounter this usage, but here's an example so you can recognize it when you do:

> Her brave *affect* couldn't completely mask the terror she was actually feeling.

TIP

You pronounce the noun form of *affect* differently from the verb form. With the noun form, you stress the first syllable, and the *a* sounds as you would if you were saying "at."

>> *Effect* may also act as a verb meaning "to cause a complete change." However, you rarely need these secondary meanings.

Between versus among

Between and *among* are two tricky prepositions that are often used incorrectly. To choose the appropriate preposition, decide how many people or things you're talking about. If the answer is two, you want *between*, as in this sentence:

> Lola was unable to choose *between* the biker magazine and *Poetry for Weightlifters.*

If you're talking about more than two people or things, *among* is the appropriate word:

> Lola strolled *among* the parked motorcycles, reading poetry aloud.

One exception: Treaties are made *between* nations, even if more than two countries sign:

> The treaty to outlaw bubble gum was negotiated *between* Libya, the United States, Russia, and Ecuador.

Continual versus continuous

Two description pairs trespass on each other's territory: *continual/continually* and *continuous/continuously*. Which pair should you use to express your meaning?

>> *Continual* and *continually* refer to events that happen over and over again, but with breaks in between each instance. *Continual* (an adjective) describes nouns, and *continually* (an adverb) describes verbs.

>> *Continuous* and *continuously* are used for situations without gaps. *Continuous* (an adjective) attaches to nouns and *continuously* (an adverb) to verbs.

Continuous noise is steady and uninterrupted, like the drone of the electric generator in your local power plant. *Continual* noise is what you hear when I go bowling. You hear silence (when I stare at the pins), a little noise (when the ball rolls down the lane), and silence again (when the ball slides into the gutter without hitting anything).

Here are a couple of examples:

Jim screamed *continuously* until Lola stuffed rags in his mouth.

Ella's *continual* attempts to impress Larry were unsuccessful, including the fruit basket she sent him on Monday and the piranha she shipped on Tuesday.

TEST ALERT

By the way, this pair had a cameo appearance on a recent standardized test. Test-takers, refer to these examples *continually* so they remain in your memory *continuously*.

Due to versus because of

According to a rule that people ignore more and more every day, here's the distinction between *due to* and *because of*:

» *Due to* describes nouns or pronouns. It may follow a linking verb if it gives information about the subject. (See Chapter 2 for a discussion of linking verbs.)

» *Because of* is a description of an action and usually answers the question "why?" (I discuss action verbs in Chapter 2 as well.)

Here are some examples:

Lola's mania for fashion is *due to* her deprived upbringing in an all-polyester household.

The bubble-gum gun that George fired is no longer being manufactured *because of* protests from the dental association.

Farther versus further

Farther refers to distance. If you need to travel farther, you have more miles to cover. *Further* doesn't refer to distance. Instead, it means "additional" and is used when discussing time, ideas, activities, and lots more. Some examples:

Mike flew *farther* than anyone else who had been kicked by the same bull.

Al needs *further* work on his teeth before the studio will approve a five-picture deal.

Lie versus lay

Whoever invented the verbs *lie* and *lay* had an evil sense of humor. Besides meaning "not to tell the truth," *lie* also means "to rest or to plop yourself down, ready for a snooze" or "to remain." *Lay* means "to put something down, to place something." Here are some examples:

> Sheila likes to *lie* down for an hour after lunch. Before she hits the couch, she *lays* a soft sheet over the upholstery.

> Roger *lies* in wait behind those bushes. When unsuspecting tourists *lay* down their picnic blankets, he swoops in and steals their lunches.

So far, this topic isn't too complicated. The truly devilish part comes in the past tense. The past tense of *lie* (to rest, to recline, to remain) is *lay*. The past tense of *lay* (to put or place) is *laid*. Check out these examples:

> Sheila *lay* down yesterday, but a car alarm disturbed her rest. She immediately went to the street and *laid* a carpet of nails in front of the offending vehicle.

> Yesterday, while Roger *lay* in wait, a police officer *laid* a hand on Roger's shoulder. "You are under arrest," intoned the cop.

Rise versus raise

Rise means "to stand," "to get out of bed," or "to move to a higher rank" under one's own power. *Raise* means "to lift something or someone else up" or "to bring up children or animals." Check out these verbs in action:

> Eggworthy *rises* when a poultry expert enters the room.

> Eggworthy is currently an apprentice, but he hopes to *rise* to the rank of master poultry-breeder some day.

> He *raises* roosters on his farm, delighting the neighbors every morning at sunrise.

> When a nest is too low, Eggworthy *raises* it to a higher shelf.

Since versus because

WARNING

Many people say *being that* to introduce a reason. Unfortunately, *being that* is a grammatical felony in the first degree; it's never acceptable in formal English. When you're explaining a reason for something, try *because* instead:

> **Wrong:** *Being that* it was Thanksgiving, Mel bought a turkey.

> **Right:** *Because* it was Thanksgiving, Mel bought a turkey.

You may like the sound of *since* in the sample sentence, and *since* is being used as a synonym for *because* more and more these days. However, grammarians prefer to use *since* only for time statements, not for reasons:

> I haven't seen the turkey *since* Herman took the ax out of the box.

Sit versus set

Sit and *set* are not interchangeable. *Sit* is what you do when you stop standing. *Set* is what you do when you place an object somewhere or you adjust or regulate something. Check out these examples:

> Anna *sits* in front of the television, even when it's broken.

> Arthur *set* the ray gun to "stun" and then *set* it carefully on the shelf.

Suppose versus supposed

Check out these sample sentences:

> Lola was *suppose* to take out the garbage, but she refused to do so.

> George is *suppose* to do all kinds of things, but of course he never does anything he is *suppose* to do.

They're both wrong. The italicized verbs represent what people hear but not what the speaker is actually trying to say. The correct verb form to use in these instances is *supposed*.

Where does *suppose* come into play? When you're musing about something in the present tense:

> I *suppose* I should take out the trash before it starts attracting wildlife.

Whether versus if

Whether and *if* both connect one idea to another in a sentence, but each is used in a different situation. Are you choosing between two alternatives? If so, select *whether* (as in *whether or not*). If you're describing a possibility, use *if*. Look at the following examples:

> George isn't sure *whether* he should activate the wind machine.

> Lulu will reach the top of Mount Everest *if* the sunny weather continues.

Who versus whom

The problem with the pronouns *who* and *whom* (and *whoever* and *whomever*) is slightly different from the problems you encounter with the other words in this section. Quite simply, no one seems to like *whom* (or *whomever*) anymore except for grammar teachers, dictionary writers, and other word geeks.

When in doubt about which word to use, you may be tempted always to go with *who* because, in speech, that's what most people use. But *whom* is still very much in vogue in formal English (the kind you use for homework, business reports, and other important documents — see Chapter 11).

Here are the rules for using *who/whoever* and *whom/whomever*:

>> You use *who* and *whoever* as subjects and to complete the meaning of linking verbs such as *is* and *seems*.

>> You use *whom* and *whomever* for all kinds of objects, such as direct objects, indirect objects, objects of prepositions, and objects of infinitives.

For information on subjects, see Chapter 2. For an explanation of objects, see Chapter 4.

Check out these sample sentences:

> *Whoever* needs help from Roger is going to wait a long time. (*Whoever* is the subject.)

> *Who* is calling Lulu at this time of night? (*Who* is the subject.)

> "I don't care *whom* you ask to the prom," exclaimed Michael. (*whom* is the direct object of the verb *ask.*)

> The trophy is for *whomever* she designates as the hot-dog eating champion. (*whomever* is the direct object of the verb *designates.*)

> For *whom* are you bellowing? (*whom* is the object of the preposition *for.*)

TEST ALERT

People have led perfectly pleasant (though grammatically incorrect) lives without knowing the stuff in this section. However, the standardized test-makers consider these topics fair game — and big game, judging from the number of questions they ask about *who* and *whom*.

A Word and a Phrase to Avoid

Irregardless of what your friends may say, you should eliminate the following word and phrase from your writing completely. If anyone offers you advice different than that, they're steering you wrong. (After you read this section, feel free to reread this paragraph and highlight the two errors. Then feel free to write a big red "F" at the top of this chapter so I'm duly chastised.)

Irregardless

WARNING

Irregardless is a grammatical no-no. I think *irregardless* is popular because it's a long word that feels good when you say it. Those r's just roll right off the tongue. Sadly, *irregardless* is not a conjunction. It's not even a word, according to the rules of formal English. Use *regardless* (not nearly so much fun to pronounce) or *despite the fact that.*

Wrong: Irregardless, we are going to eat you, you turkey!

Right: Regardless, we are going to eat you, you turkey!

Also right: Despite the fact that you are a tough old bird, we are going to eat you, you turkey!

Different than

How many times have you heard this sentence?

Prepositions are different than other parts of speech.

Okay, never. But I bet you've heard (and maybe used) the expression *different than* lots of times. I hate to break the bad news, but I must. *Different than* is never correct. What you want is *different from.* The explanation behind this truth is fascinating if you love grammar so much that you dream about it at night. In a nutshell, *from* is a preposition and *than* isn't. In this phrase, you need a preposition.

I'll stop right there and spare you the fascinating details. Just know that you shouldn't ever write "different than" in a situation that requires formal English. Here's what you want instead:

Prepositions are *different from* other parts of speech.

Chapter **10**

Tackling Other Troublemakers

In this chapter, I shine the light on a trio of troublemakers so they'll never trip you up again. First, I show you how to create plural nouns. Regular nouns are easy to pluralize, but some nouns come with their own set of rules. Next, I introduce you to prepositions, explain how to use them, and put you on high alert for common problems writers encounter with them. Finally, I wrestle with double negatives so you won't never put them in your writing no more. (That was a triple negative, in case you were wondering.)

Creating Noun Plurals

In Chapter 2, I introduce you to nouns, which are the subjects of most sentences. (Pronouns, which I examine in Chapter 3, can also serve as subjects.) Nouns are people, places, things, and ideas, and you can change most of them from singular to plural pretty easily. Garden-variety nouns form plurals by adding the letter s. Check out Table 10-1 for some examples.

TABLE 10-1 Creating Plurals with Regular Nouns

Singular	Plural
xylophone	xylophones
nerd	nerds
eyebrow	eyebrows

Singular nouns that end in *s, sh, ch,* and *x* form plurals by adding *es.* Some examples appear in Table 10-2.

TABLE 10-2 Creating Plurals with Regular Nouns Ending in *s, sh, ch,* and *x*

Singular	Plural
kiss	kisses
bush	bushes
grinch	grinches
box	boxes

The -ies and -ys have it

If a noun ends in *y* and the letter before the *y* is a vowel (*a, e, i, o,* or *u*), just add *s* to form the plural. For examples, see Table 10-3.

TABLE 10-3 Creating Plurals with Regular Nouns Ending in a Vowel plus *y*

Singular	Plural
monkey	monkeys
turkey	turkeys
day	days
boy	boys

If the noun ends in *y* but the letter before the *y* is not a vowel, form the plural by changing the *y* to *i* and adding *es.* For examples, see Table 10-4.

TABLE 10-4 Creating Plurals with Regular Nouns Ending in a Consonant plus *y*

Singular	Plural
story	stories
mystery	mysteries
pinky	pinkies

WARNING

Never change the spelling of a name when you make it plural. The plural of *Sammy* is *Sammys*, not *Sammies*. Ditto with *BlackBerrys*. (No *BlackBerries*, please.)

Gooses? Childs? Forming irregular plurals

This topic wouldn't be any fun without irregulars, now would it? Irregulars are a pain and, to be blunt, require memorization. I can't list every irregular plural in this chapter, but you need to know that they exist. If your ear tells you that the way you've formed a plural just isn't working, consult your dictionary. Table 10-5 gives you some common examples of irregular plurals.

TABLE 10-5 Examples of Irregular Plurals

Singular	Plural
foot	feet
tooth	teeth
goose	geese
knife	knives
leaf	leaves
mouse	mice
man	men
woman	women
child	children

(continued)

TABLE 10-5 *(continued)*

Singular	Plural
person	people
sheep	sheep
fish	fish
deer	deer

Making plurals with hyphenated nouns

If you intend to insult your in-laws, you may as well do so with the correct plural form. You form the plural of hyphenated nouns by adding *s* or *es* to the important word, not to the add-on. These words are all plurals:

>> mothers-in-law

>> brothers-in-law

>> vice-presidents

>> secretaries-general

REMEMBER

You may hear references to "attorney generals." But keep in mind that an attorney general is a lawyer, not a military officer. Therefore, *attorney* is the important part of this title, and it's a noun. The *general* is a description — a reference to the rank of the *attorney*. To form a plural, you deal with the noun, not with the descriptive word. Therefore, you have one *attorney general* and two or more *attorneys general*.

Perfecting Prepositions

How does the cliché go? Little things mean a lot? Whoever said that was probably talking about prepositions. These guys — some of which are the shortest words in the language — pack a punch in your sentences. Unfortunately, prepositions also attract mistakes. In this section I explain prepositions and show you how to avoid the pitfalls associated with them.

Expressing relationships

Imagine that you encounter two nouns: *elephant* and *book*. How many ways can you connect the two nouns to express different ideas? Here are just a few:

the book *about* the elephant

the book *by* the elephant

the book *in front of* the elephant

the book *under* the elephant

REMEMBER

The italicized words relate two nouns to each other. These relationship words are called prepositions. A *preposition* is any word or group of words that relates a noun or a pronoun to another word in the sentence.

When I was in grammar school, I had to memorize a list of prepositions. I was so terrified of Sister Saint Vincent, my seventh-grade teacher, that I made the list part of my being. I don't think memorizing prepositions is worth the time, but a familiarity with them would be nice. Therefore, I offer this list of some common prepositions:

>> about

>> above

>> according to

>> across

>> after

>> against

>> along

>> amid

>> among

>> around

>> at

>> before

>> behind

>> below

>> beside

>> besides

>> between

>> beyond

>> by

>> concerning

>> down

>> during

>> except

>> for

>> from

>> in

>> into

>> like

» of		» underneath
» off		» until
» on		» up
» over		» upon
» past		» with
» since		» within
» through		» without
» toward		

Eyeing the objects of prepositional phrases

REMEMBER

Prepositions never travel alone; they're always with one or more objects. A *prepositional phrase* consists of a preposition and an object. In the examples in the preceding section, the object of each preposition is *elephant.* The object of a preposition is always a noun or a pronoun, or perhaps one or two of each. (A *pronoun* is a word that takes the place of a noun, such as *him* for *Eggworthy.*) Here's an example:

In the afternoon, the snow pelted Eggworthy on his little bald head.

This sentence has two prepositions: *in* and *on. Afternoon* is the object of the preposition *in,* and *head* is the object of the preposition *on.* Why is the object *head* and not *little* or *bald?* You can throw out a few things inside a prepositional phrase — mainly descriptive words. Check out these variations on the phrase *of the elephant:*

of the *apologetic* elephant

of the *antagonizingly argumentative* elephant

When you weed through the descriptions, each phrase is still talking about just one noun: *elephant.* Only nouns and pronouns are allowed to be objects of the preposition — not adjectives or adverbs (which I discuss in Chapter 6).

Identifying the objects of prepositions

TIP

All objects answer the questions *whom?* or *what?* To find the object of a preposition, ask *whom?* or *what?* after the preposition. For example, in this sentence you see two prepositional phrases:

> Marilyn thought that the selection of the elephant for the show was quite unfair.

The first preposition is *of. Of* what? *Of* the *elephant. Elephant* is the object of the preposition *of.* The second preposition is *for. For* what? *For* the *show. Show* is the object of the preposition *for.*

Paying attention to prepositions

Why bother paying attention to prepositions at all? I can think of a couple key reasons.

When you're checking subject-verb pairs, you need to identify and then ignore the prepositional phrases. The prepositional phrases are distractions. If you don't ignore them, you may end up matching the verb to the wrong word. (See Chapter 2 for more information on subject-verb agreement.)

You may also find it helpful to recognize prepositional phrases because sometimes when you're trying to find an adjective or an adverb, the answer is a prepositional phrase. Don't panic. You haven't done anything wrong. Simply know that a prepositional phrase may do the same job as a single-word adjective or adverb. (See Chapter 6 for more on adjectives and adverbs.)

TEST ALERT

A few questions in the SAT Writing and the ACT English tortures — sorry, I mean *tests* — revolve around prepositions. You may encounter a misused preposition (*to* instead of *with*, for example) or a situation in which another part of speech grabs a preposition's rightful spot (*different than* instead of *different from*, perhaps).

Are you talking to I? Matching prepositions and pronouns

WARNING

A big preposition pitfall is pronouns (see Chapter 3). Only certain pronouns (called *object pronouns*) can act as objects of prepositions. If you use the wrong pronoun as the object of a preposition, the grammar cops will be on your case.

REMEMBER

The object pronouns are *me, you, him, her, it, us, them, whom,* and *whomever.* Take a look at some sentences with a pronoun as the object of a preposition:

> *Among* Bill, Harry, and *me* there is no contest. (*Me* is one of the objects of the preposition *among.*)

> *Without them,* the bridge will fall out of Cedric's mouth. (*Them* is the object of the preposition *without.* In case you're wondering, it's a dental bridge.)

> Lester added an amendment to the bill *concerning us.* (*Us* is the object of the preposition *concerning.*)

WARNING

One of the most common errors in the use of object pronouns involves the prepositional phrases *between you and I* and *between you and me.* Which one is correct? The phrase is *between you and me. Between* is the preposition. *You and me* are the objects of the preposition. *Me* is an object pronoun. *I* is a subject pronoun, so you can't use it here.

Test your pronoun knowledge. Which sentence is correct?

> A. According to Elton and she, the elephant's nose is simply too long.

> B. According to Elton and her, the elephant's nose is simply too long.

Answer: Sentence B is correct. *According to* is the preposition. The object of the preposition is *Elton and her. Her* is an object pronoun. (*She* is a subject pronoun.)

Most of the tough pronoun choices involve a sentence with a preposition that has more than one object (*Elton and her,* for example). Your ear for grammar will probably tell you the correct pronoun when the sentence has a single pronoun object. You probably wouldn't say *according to she* because it sounds funny.

TIP

If a sentence has a preposition with more than one object, try this tip: Cover one of the objects with your finger and then say the sentence. Does it sound right?

A good part of speech to end a sentence with?

As I write this paragraph, global warming is increasing, the Pacific Ocean sports a trash pile twice the size of Texas, and reality TV shows are still on the air. In the midst of these truly troubling events, some people still walk around worrying about where to put a preposition. Specifically, they worry about whether ending a sentence with a preposition is acceptable. Let me illustrate the problem:

> Tell me whom he spoke *about.*

> Tell me *about* whom he spoke.

REMEMBER

Here's the verdict: Both sentences are correct for most people and even for most grammarians. However, if you're writing for someone who loves to tsk-tsk about the decline of proper English, avoid placing a preposition at the end of a sentence.

Deleting Double Negatives

In some languages, the more negatives the better. In English, two negatives are a no-no. (By the way, no-no is *not* a double negative; it's just slang for something that's prohibited.) Here I explain some of the trickiest forms of double trouble.

If you think this is a useless grammar rule, think again. A double-negative mistake can completely wreck your sentence, because in English, two negatives make a positive.

TIP

The simplest way to correct double-negative errors is to eliminate one of the negatives. For example, instead of saying, "I haven't never been to California," say, "I haven't been to California" or "I've never been to California." Or just go to California and eliminate the issue altogether.

One of the most common double negatives doesn't look like one: *can't help but.* Consider an example:

> Eggworthy *can't help but* act in that dramatic style because he was trained by a real ham.

The *not* (inside the word *can't*) and the *but* both express negative ideas. Use one or the other — not both:

> Eggworthy *can't help acting* in that dramatic style because he was trained by a real ham.

WARNING

Another phrase to avoid in formal English is *can't hardly. Can't* is short for *cannot*, which contains the negative *not. Hardly* is another negative word. If you combine them, you say the opposite of what you intend — the positive instead of the negative. Here's an example:

> According to Lola, Ella can't hardly wait until her divorce becomes final.

What the writer thinks the sentence means: Ella is eager for her divorce to become final.

What the sentence actually means: Ella can wait. (The palace is comfy, and Larry isn't around much.)

Right: Ella can hardly wait until her divorce becomes final.

Also right: Ella can't wait until her divorce becomes final.

IN THIS CHAPTER

» Figuring out your audience first

» Putting your computer's grammar check in place

» Beefing up your verbs

» Creating concise, exciting writing

» Communicating electronically

Chapter **11**

Improving Your Writing

A ll the grammar rules in the world mean nothing if no one wants to read what you've written. As a writer, you have multiple goals: You need to communicate with a specific audience in a way that's appropriate, compelling, clear, and concise. This chapter offers tips for doing just that, regardless of whether you're writing an e-mail, an annual report, or an 80-page thesis.

Identifying Your Audience

Good grammar is essential, but *good* is tough to pin down because the language of choice depends on your situation. For instance, imagine that you're hungry. What do you say?

Will you accompany me to the dining room?

Do you feel like getting a sandwich?

These statements illustrate two types of English: formal English and conversational English. Before you can choose which English to use, you need to know your audience.

Keeping it formal

At the pickiest end of the language spectrum, formal English displays the fact that you have an advanced vocabulary, a knowledge of etiquette, and a command of standard rules of English usage. You may use formal English when you have less power, importance, and/or status than the other person in the conversation. Formal English shows that you've trotted out your best behavior in his or her honor. You may also speak or write in formal English when you have *more* power, importance, and/or status than the other person. In that case, you want to impress, to create a tone of dignity, or to provide a suitable role model for someone who is still learning. Situations that call for formal English include

>> Business letters or e-mails (from or between businesses as well as from individuals to businesses)

>> Communications to teachers

>> Homework

>> Important conversations (for example, job interviews, college interviews, parole hearings, congressional inquiries, and so on)

>> Letters or e-mails to government officials

>> Office memos or e-mails

>> Reports

>> Speeches, presentations, and oral reports

All the grammar lessons in this book deal with formal English because that's where the problems are fiercest and the rewards for knowledge are greatest.

Knowing when conversational English will work

Conversational English doesn't stray too far from your English class rules, but it does break some. You can relax, but not completely. It's the tone of most everyday speech, especially between equals. Conversational English is — no shock here — usually for conversations, but here are some writing situations when it's acceptable:

- **>>** Comments in Internet chat rooms, bulletin boards, and so on
- **>>** Friendly letters to relatives
- **>>** Notes, e-mails, instant messages, and texts to friends

Conversational English has a breezy sound. You find more contractions (*don't, I'll, would've*, and so forth). You may also skip words (*Got a minute? Be there soon!*), especially if you're writing in electronic media with a tight space requirement. (For more on electronic communication, see "Writing for Electronic Media" later in this chapter.)

In written form, conversational English relaxes the punctuation rules, too. Sentences run together, dashes connect all sorts of things, and half sentences pop up regularly. I'm using conversational English to write this book because I'm pretending that I'm chatting with you rather than teaching grammar in a classroom situation.

Cutting Ties with Your Computer Grammar Checker

Your best friend may tell you that learning correct grammar in the third millennium is irrelevant because computer grammar checkers make human knowledge obsolete. Your friend is wrong.

WARNING

It's comforting to think that a little green or red line will tell you when you've made an error and that a quick mouse click will show you the path to perfection. Comforting, but unreal. English has a half million words, and you can arrange those words a couple gazillion ways. No program can catch all your mistakes, and most programs identify errors that aren't actually wrong.

Spelling is also a problem. Every time I type *verbal*, the computer squawks. But *verbal* — a grammar term meaning a word that comes from a verb but doesn't function as a verb — is a real word. (In fact, I devote a whole section to verbals later in this chapter.) Nor can the computer tell the difference between *homonyms*: words that sound alike but have different meanings and spellings. For example, if I type

Eye through the bawl at hymn, but it went threw the window pain instead.

the computer underlines nothing. However, I was actually trying to say

I threw the ball at him, but it went through the window pane instead.

The computer knows some grammar and spelling, but you have to know the rest.

REMEMBER

Giving Your Writing Punch with Great Verbs

To engage your reader, you want to create active, energetic writing. The best way to do so is to choose active, energetic verbs. In this section, I show you how.

Staying active

Verbs can have two voices: active and passive. Take a look at these two examples:

"The window *was broken* yesterday," reported Eggworthy, carefully hiding his baseball bat under the sofa.

"I *broke* the window yesterday," reported Eggworthy, regretfully handing his baseball bat to his mother.

How do the two versions differ? Grammatically, Eggworthy's statement in the first sentence focuses on the receiver of the action, the *window*, which received the action of *breaking*. The verb is *passive* because the subject isn't the person or thing doing the action but instead the person or thing receiving the action. In sentence two, the verb is in active voice because the subject (*I*) performed the action (*broke*). When the subject is acting or being, the verb is *active*.

Here are some active and passive verb examples:

> Lulu *gives* a free-tattoo coupon to Lola. (active)
>
> Lola *is persuaded* by Lulu to get a tattoo. (passive)
>
> Roger *persuades* Lulu to visit the tattoo parlor too. (active)
>
> Lulu *is tattooed* by Lola. (passive)

TIP

Unless you're trying to hide something, or unless you truly don't know the facts, you should make your writing as specific as possible. Specifics reside in active voice. Compare these two sentences:

> The president of the Egg-Lovers' Club *was murdered* yesterday.
>
> Sir Francis Bacon *murdered* the president of the Egg-Lovers' Club yesterday.

Clearly, the active-verb sentence provides more information: It tells you the murderer's name. Knowing is usually better than not knowing, and active voice — which generally provides more facts — is usually better than passive voice.

Active voice is also better than passive because active voice tends to use fewer words to say the same thing. Compare the following sentences:

> Lulu was failed by the teacher because the grammar book was torn up by Lulu before it was ever opened. (20 words)
>
> The teacher failed Lulu because Lulu tore up the grammar book before opening it. (14 words)

If you're writing a letter or an essay, switching from passive to active voice may save you one-third of your words — and therefore, one-third of the reader's energy and patience.

TEST ALERT

Some questions on the SAT and ACT ask you to revise a sentence by choosing the best of five possible versions. Fairly often, the correct answer changes the passive verb of the original to active voice.

Knowing when "there is" a problem

In my writing class, I always ask the students to describe a standard school chair. Inevitably, I read sentences like these:

> There is a curved seat.
>
> There are five slats on the back.

Nothing's wrong with these sentences. They're grammatically correct, and they're accurate. But I bet they made you yawn. *There is* and *there are*, as well as their cousins — *there was, there will be, there has been*, and others — are standard (and therefore boring) expressions. How about swapping them for something stronger? Here you go:

> The seat curves to fit your bottom.
>
> Five slats support your back.

TEST ALERT

In a writing sample for the SAT or other standardized test, graders watch for sophisticated usage. They want to see that you can manipulate language. *There is/are* sentences aren't very sophisticated, though they can sometimes be useful. When you find yourself constructing a sentence this way, pause. Can you come up with a more interesting verb?

Recognizing that your writing "has" issues

If they're overused, forms of *to have* can also put your reader to sleep faster than a sedative. Sometimes, nothing works better than *to have*, but too often, *has, had,* or *have* ends up in a sentence because the writer is too lazy to think of something more creative. Try changing

> The chair has a shiny surface.
>
> The slats have rounded edges as big as my finger.

to

> The chair shone under the fluorescent light.
>
> The rounded edges fit my finger perfectly.

Okay, I added some information to the second set, but you see my point. *Shone* and *fit* are more interesting than *has* and *have*. Plus, after you plop in a good verb, other ideas follow, and the whole sentence improves.

Letting your subjects do more than "say" and "walk"

To say and *to walk* are fine, upstanding members of the verb community, but they don't give you much information. Why *say* when you can *declare, scream, whisper, hint, bellow, assert, remark* or do any one of the zillions of alternatives available to you when you're describing communication? For movement, consider *stroll, saunter, plod, strut, rush, speed, zigzag*, and — well, you get the point. Look for verbs that go beyond the basics and add shades of meaning to your sentence. Here are some before-and-after sentence sets to illustrate how more specific verbs pep up your sentences:

> **Before:** Heidi said that she was tired of climbing mountains.
>
> **After:** Heidi murmured that she was tired of climbing mountains. (Here Heidi is a bit shy or perhaps fearful.)
>
> **Another after:** Heidi roared that she was tired of climbing mountains. (In this sentence, no one is going to mess with Heidi — not without a struggle!)
>
> **Before:** Heidi's hiking partner walked away from her.
>
> **After:** Heidi's hiking partner edged away from her. (The partner knows that Heidi is in one of her moods, and trouble is on the way.)
>
> **Another after:** Heidi's hiking partner stomped away from her. (Now the partner is angry!)

TIP

Your word-processing program probably has a built-in *thesaurus*: a reference work that lists synonyms for words, including most verbs. You can also buy a thesaurus in book form. If you're looking over your writing and need some spicier verbs, a thesaurus can suggest some alternatives.

But be cautious: Certain verbs may be similar but not exactly the same. For example, the list for *stroll* includes *ramble* and *promenade*. You may *ramble* (or *amble*, another verb on this list) without a fixed destination or purpose. If you *promenade*, you're probably also in recreational mode, but this time you have an audience. Bottom line: Don't insert a verb (or any other word) into your sentence unless you're sure you know what it means.

Deleting All That's Extra

I live in Manhattan, an island surrounded by water. My 17-story apartment building is tall. It was built many years ago in 1929. I work as a teacher in a school. I write Dummies books about grammar, which explain grammar to readers. I will also consider jumping from the roof of my tall apartment building if I have to write any more boring, repetitive, say-the-same-thing-at-least-twice sentences like these.

Okay, I believe I made my point. Sentences stuffed with filler sound silly and condescend to the reader. I mean, really. *An island surrounded by water* — that's clever. What surrounds other islands? Bagels? My *Dummies books about grammar explain grammar to readers.* There's a shock. I'm sure you thought my grammar books explained tai chi or llama-raising. And after I wrote *repetitive*, I didn't have to tack on *say-the-same-thing-at-least-twice.* One word said it all.

Should you care about wordy, repetitive sentences? For several reasons, you should care very much:

>> If you say the same thing over and over again, your readers or listeners tune you out. Why would they pay close attention? If they miss something, they assume you'll go over the same ground again.

>> Repetition wastes time, one of the most valuable commodities on earth. As one of my Dummies editors once remarked, "Say it and move on. Our readers are busy!"

>> If you're writing under pressure — a school assignment or a work project, perhaps — you need fewer minutes to accomplish your task if you don't repeat yourself.

» Concise writing sounds strong and confident. Take a look at this sentence:

In my opinion, I think that homework should possibly be considered for banning.

Compare that clunker with this sentence:

Homework should be banned.

Do I have to ask which version sounds more forceful? Version 1 fumbles around. Version 2 hits you right on the nose.

TEST ALERT A frequent flyer on the SAT Writing and the ACT English tests is repetition. The test gnomes want to know that you can pare down your prose to its leanest state without sacrificing meaning.

Spicing Up Boring Sentences

Which paragraph sounds better?

Michael purchased a new spy camera. The camera was smaller than a grain of rice. Michael gave the camera to Lola. Lola is rather forgetful. She is especially forgetful now. Lola is planning a trip to Antarctica. Lola accidentally mixed the camera into her rice casserole along with bean sprouts and orange marmalade. The camera baked for 45 minutes. The camera became quite tender. Michael unknowingly ate the camera.

Michael purchased a new spy camera that was smaller than a grain of rice. Michael gave the camera to Lola, who is rather forgetful, especially now that she is planning a trip to Antarctica. Accidentally mixed into Lola's rice casserole along with bean sprouts and orange marmalade, the camera baked for 45 minutes. Michael unknowingly ate the camera, which was quite tender.

I'm going to take a guess that you said the second paragraph is better. It's a bit shorter (62 words instead of 69), but length isn't the issue. The first paragraph is composed of short, choppy sentences. The second one flows. Grammatically, the difference between the two is simple: The second paragraph has more subordinate clauses and verbals than the first.

TIP

You don't need to know how to find or label clauses or verbals. However, you should read your writing aloud from time to time to check how it sounds. The old saying "variety is the spice of life" applies to writing. Use this checklist to see whether your writing could use a little hot pepper:

>> Do all your sentences follow the same basic pattern — subject-verb or subject-verb-complement?

>> Have you strung a lot of short sentences together with *and* or a similar joining word?

>> Are all your sentences more or less the same length?

If you answered yes to one or more of the preceding questions, a trip to the spice rack is in order. In this section, with a minimum of grammatical labels, I suggest some ways to add flavor to blah sentences.

The clause that refreshes

Have you ever seen those diet ads on late-night television? The before picture shows someone who has apparently eaten a rain forest, and the after picture displays a toothpick-thin body. In this section I provide some before-and-after sentences. No diets are involved — just a change from boring to interesting. My insertions are subordinate (or *dependent*) clauses, which are italicized. (Subordinate clauses can't stand on their own as complete sentences; see Chapter 4.)

> **Boring before version:** Max sat on a tuffet. Max did not know that he was sitting on a tuffet. Max had never seen a tuffet before. He was quite comfortable. Then Ms. Muffet came in and caused trouble.

> **Exciting after version:** Max, *who was sitting on a tuffet,* didn't know *what a tuffet was because he had never seen one before. Until Ms. Muffet came in and caused trouble,* Max was quite comfortable.

Doesn't the "after" paragraph sound better? It's three words shorter (32 instead of 35 words), but more important than length is the number of sentences. The before paragraph has five, and the after paragraph has two. Tucking more than one idea into a sentence saves words and makes your writing less choppy.

Verbally speaking

Verbals are verb forms that don't act as verbs in a sentence. To combine ideas and make your writing more interesting, you can use three types of verbals:

» **Gerunds:** Verbs that end in *-ing* and act as nouns. Many of the chapter titles and headings in this book start with gerunds. "Improving Your Writing," for example, is a gerund phrase that starts with a gerund.

» **Infinitives:** The word *to* plus a verb, such as *to be, to drive,* and *to prance.* Technically, infinitives are never verbs, even though everyone — yours truly included — tends to refer to them as such.

» **Participles:** These critters are parts of verbs (hence their name) that may have endings such as *-ed, -en,* or (like a gerund) *-ing.* Participles describe nouns and pronouns, which means they act like adjectives (see Chapter 6). One quick example: In the sentence *Ella is exhausted,* the word *exhausted* is a participle. (It's a form of the verb *exhaust* that describes Ella.)

Consider a verbal in action. Start with two run-of-the-mill sentences:

Betsy's team lost its 450th game in a row. Betsy thought seriously about whether she should bribe the umpire.

Nothing's wrong with these sentences. But how might you approach the same information differently to spice up your writing? Here's one possibility:

Betsy gave *bribing the umpire* serious consideration when her team lost its 450th game in a row.

You may identify the word *bribing* as a verb, but look at the rest of the sentence. Your subject is *Betsy,* and your verb is *gave.* Where does that leave *bribing?* In this sentence, it's a gerund.

Are verbals required elements in your writing? No, but think of them as one more color in your crayon box when you're creating a picture. Here's a before-and-after example:

Boring before version: Lulu smacked Larry. Larry had stolen the sacred toe hoop from Lulu's parrot. The sacred toe hoop was discovered 100 years ago. Lulu's parrot likes to sharpen his beak on it.

Exciting after version: *Smacking Larry* is Lulu's way of telling Larry that he shouldn't have stolen the sacred toe hoop from her parrot. *Discovered 100 years ago,* the toe hoop serves *to sharpen the parrot's beak.*

Labels for those who care: *Smacking Lulu* is a gerund; *discovered 100 years ago* is a participle; *to sharpen the parrot's beak* is an infinitive.

Writing for Electronic Media

You may send dozens (even hundreds) of electronic messages — whether tweets, texts, or e-mails — each day. Why do I bother including a section in this book on media that most people are already so comfortable using? Because most of those *most people* don't spend nearly enough time thinking about grammar when writing electronically. In fact, I'd wager that most people don't even proofread their communications before hitting "send" on their computers, cell phones, or whatever.

REMEMBER

If you're chatting with your mom or best friend, you can be as lax as you'd like. But if you're writing an e-mail or text to a boss, teacher, or other authority figure, you need to treat that communication just as seriously as one that's submitted on paper.

Scoping your audience

Earlier in this chapter, I explain the need to identify your audience before writing anything. You may assume you never need to write in formal English when your means of communication is a BlackBerry, but that's not true. The medium is irrelevant when determining how formal your writing should be. What matters — as always — is your audience. Consider these guidelines:

>> **Focus on the identity of the person receiving the message.** If he or she is a friend who can practically read your mind, formal English isn't necessary. Abbreviations and half-sentences are probably fine, and you don't need to worry about capitalization and punctuation.

The less friendly the relationship, the more correct your language and grammar should be. If you're writing to someone you've met only once or twice, don't chop out letters or words unless you know that the recipient appreciates informality. Stick to the normal rules for capitalization and punctuation unless you're sure that the message receiver is comfortable with nonstandard English.

>> **Consider your relative power.** If you're the boss, you make the rules. Your subordinates aren't going to point out that you lowercased a word that should be in caps — not if they want to keep working for you! But if your message is going up the chain of command, choose formal English.

Most teachers favor formal English. Follow grammar rules when you write to anyone in the academic world.

REMEMBER

>> **Think about the impression you're trying to make.** If you're writing to a potential client, formal language may show respect and care. On the other hand, if you've got an antsy client — the type who wants the work done yesterday, if not sooner — a few dropped words or characters may give the impression that you're speeding along on the client's behalf, too busy for such niceties as commas and periods.

REMEMBER

Save abbreviations such as "ttyl" (*talk to you later*), "lol" (*laughing out loud*), and "ctn" (*can't talk now*) for your "bff" (*best friend forever*). However, some abbreviations are acceptable in business or academic writing. For example, you may begin a message with "FYI" (*for your information*) and ask for a reply "ASAP" (*as soon as possible*). If the abbreviation appears in a dictionary, it's probably okay unless you're writing in an extremely formal situation.

Being clear and concise

No matter who the recipient is, you have to get your point across. The screens and keyboards of smart phones and hand-held devices are as tiny as low-calorie cookies, so sending or reading a long letter isn't comfortable. Plus, depending on the device and cost structure of your carrier, you may pay extra if you're not concise. Some formats even have a character limit. The conclusion is obvious: Make your messages as short as possible to avoid eye and finger fatigue.

REMEMBER

Compressing your thoughts into the smallest space doesn't get you off the hook when it comes to grammar, however. Remember one rule, no matter what you're writing with, on, or to: Be clear!

Your reader has to understand what you mean or your message is a failure. With that principle in mind, check out the following guidelines.

Dropping words

When every character counts (such as when you're texting), you may at times break the "complete sentence" rule. (See Chapter 4 for a thorough explanation of what constitutes a complete sentence.) The most common cut is the subject of a sentence. For example, you may type

> Left meeting early. No progress.

to someone who knows that despite having an early dinner date, you attended a session of that learned (and imaginary) society, Grammarians for Punctuation Reform. However, don't omit a subject unless you're absolutely sure that no confusion may result.

TIP

Articles (*a, an, the*) and conjunctions (words that join, such as *and, or,* and *but*) can often be omitted. Just be aware that the resulting message sounds rushed and at times strange. Can you imagine typing, "I went to bar"? Somehow, *the* makes a big difference.

Dropping punctuation and capital letters

Some hand-held devices automatically correct your typing by inserting capital letters and a period after you've typed two spaces. Others don't. I realize that capital letters may be a pain to type when you're on the go, but I'm in favor of that little extra effort. Ditto for periods. Yes, some people text

> saw helen after the meeting

and civilization as we know it hasn't yet crumbled. But don't you like this version better?

> Saw Helen after the meeting.

Or

I saw Helen after the meeting.

Okay, maybe you don't. But some people, including me, do. Why take a chance on offending your reader?

WARNING

Dropping a comma or a period usually isn't crucial. However, don't skip anything that adds meaning, such as question marks. Take a look at these two text messages:

Dinner at 5

Dinner at 5?

Obviously, they express two different ideas. The first assumes attendance, and the second is an invitation.

Structuring an e-mail message

In this section, I walk you through the parts of an e-mail, explaining the best format to use when you're writing to someone who expects good grammar.

The heading

Atop every e-mail is a little box with a heading, which includes a subject line — the title of your e-mail. Most people follow standard capitalization rules for the subject line (see Chapter 8). Whatever you do, be sure to proofread your subject line before sending the message. You don't want a message with a messed-up title being replied to, forwarded, and spread to your entire office.

The greeting

The message often begins with a greeting (in English-teacher terminology, a *salutation*). These are all acceptable greetings, complete with punctuation:

Dear Ms. Snodgrass, or **Dear Ms. Snodgrass:** (The one with the comma is less formal. Begin the message on the following line.)

To Whom It May Concern: (This one always has a colon and is ultra-formal. Begin the message on the following line.)

Hi, Lola. or **Hi, Ms. Snodgrass.** (Use these forms for friends and acquaintances. Begin the message right after the period, not on the next line.)

Some writers drop the greeting altogether. No problem, unless you happen to be writing to traditionalists, who prefer the time-honored formats.

The body

When writing your message, follow the grammar rules outlined in the rest of this book, matching your level of formality to the identity of the person you're writing to.

The closing

If you haven't bothered with a greeting, don't worry about a closing either, unless you want to "sign" your name at the end of the message. If you like a big send-off, try one of these:

Best, (short for "best regards" and good for formal and informal e-mails)

Sincerely, (formal)

See you soon, (informal)

Hope to hear from you, (somewhere between formal and informal)

Regards, (formal and a little old-fashioned)

You can also close your message simply by typing your name (*Lola* or *Ms. Snodgrass*) or your initials (*LS* for "Lola Snodgrass").

Proofreading before you send

REMEMBER

Type carefully, and reread what you typed before sending the message. (You may also want to run spell check — just don't rely on it completely.) Some people easily decode mistyped words as they read, but do you want to risk having your *wrods* — oops, I mean *words* — turn into a puzzle? And even if your reader can understand what you've written, do you really want to leave your reader with the impression that he or she means so little to you that you couldn't bother typing 17 little words correctly?

Chapter **12**

Ten Ways to Improve Your Grammar Every Day

This book helps you learn grammar, but it's not the only way to improve your communication skills. Lots of other resources can also help you in your quest for perfect language. In this chapter, I suggest ten ways you can improve your grammar just by making small changes to your daily routine.

Pick Up a Good Book

You probably won't get far with *Biker Babes and Their Turn-ons* or *You're a Butthead: The Sequel to Snot-Nose.* But good books usually contain good writing, and if you read some, pretty soon your own speech and writing will improve.

TIP

How do you know whether a particular volume contains good writing? Check the reviews, ask the bookstore clerk, or read the comments on the book's jacket. Classics are always a good choice, but you may also find modern texts, both fiction and nonfiction, written according to the best grammar rules.

The point is to expose your mind to proper English by reading a few pages every day. When you read, you hear the author's voice, and you become accustomed to proper language. After a while, correct grammar sounds natural to you, and you detect nonstandard English more easily.

If your schedule is so hectic that you can't find time for even a few pages a day, listen to books on tape when you're in the car. You'll still benefit from the exposure to good writing.

Read the Newspaper

Well, read *some* newspapers. Years ago I started to "pay" my students one point for each grammar error they found in print. I eventually had to rule out a couple of publications because it was just too easy to gather material. Opt for periodicals such as *The New York Times, The Washington Post,* or *The Wall Street Journal* instead. Read news articles with a grammarian's eye, absorbing how the writer expresses an idea.

Sample Some Magazines

If all the words in the magazines you read are in bubbles above brightly colored drawings, you may not find complete sentences and proper pronoun usage. However, most published writers use at least the fundamentals of good grammar, and you can learn a lot from reading publications aimed at an educated audience.

How do you know whether a publication is aimed at an educated audience? Check the articles. If they seem to address issues that you associate with thoughtful readers, you're okay. Need some suggestions? Check out *The Atlantic Monthly, Harper's, National Geographic, The New Yorker,* or *Vanity Fair.* Reading well-written magazine articles gives you some models of reasonably correct grammar. And, as a side effect, you'll learn something.

Delve into Strunk and White

The best book ever written on writing is *The Elements of Style* (Allyn and Bacon). This book is so tiny that it fits into your shirt pocket. Authors William Strunk, Jr. and E. B. White (yes, the fellow who wrote *Charlotte's Web* and *Stuart Little*) tackle a few grammar issues and make important points about style.

REMEMBER

How can such a little book become part of your daily routine? You'll spend an hour reading it and a lifetime absorbing its lessons. Whenever you write — whether an e-mail or a 30-page report — ask yourself what Strunk and White would do.

Surf the Web

I can't leave this one out, though the Internet contains as many traps as it does guiding lights. Type *grammar* in a search engine and press enter. Sit back and prepare yourself for a flood of sites explaining the rules of grammar. Some sites are very good; some are horrible. University- or school-sponsored Web sites are usually a safe bet.

TIP

Not sure where to start? Check out Grammar Girl at `http://grammar.quickanddirtytips.com` or Common Errors in English Usage at `www.wsu.edu/~brians/errors/index.html`.

Review Style Manuals

What's a *style manual?* It's a publication that contains more grammar rules than any human being needs to know, and when you're writing a paper or report, it's your bible. Your teacher, boss, or other authority figure will tell you which style manual to follow. (If not, you should ask.) For example, your teacher may ask you to follow *MLA style,* which means that you use the rules published by the Modern Language Association. Your boss may prefer *The Chicago Manual of Style* or *The New York Times Manual of Style and Usage.* Or your workplace may have its own internal manual of style, which trumps all others.

Confession time: I don't expect or even *want* you to read a style manual every day. Even professional grammarians don't like style manuals that much. But these resources are great to have on hand whenever you write something substantial because they tell you in detail where to put every punctuation mark ever invented, what to capitalize, how to address an ambassador, and lots of other things that you never really wanted to know.

Watch High-Quality TV Shows

When I say to watch *high-quality* TV shows, I'm not talking about programs with audio tracks that are mostly grunts, such as wrestling. I'm referring to shows in which people converse. Programs on the nerd networks are a good bet. You know the shows I mean — the ones whose producers assume that the audience wants to learn something. The screen has a lot of talking heads (images of commentators, not the rock band) with subtitles explaining why each is an expert. Pay attention to the words. Don't expect to pick up the finer points of grammar on TV, but you can get some daily practice with the basics.

Peruse the News

News broadcasts on radio, TV, and the Internet are fine sources of literate (okay, semi-literate on some networks) role models. In just a few minutes each day, you can train your ear for grammar at the same time that you find out about current events. Just think of the advantage when you need a pick-up line. Instead of "Come here often?" or "What's your sign?" you can mention the West's diplomatic stance on Iran. (On second thought, maybe you should stick to astrology.)

Not sure where to find a good news broadcast? Try tuning into a local radio station that carries National Public Radio programming.

Download Podcasts

Though the Internet has been blamed for the death of language by (in my opinion) hysterical, anti-technology types, you can find terrific material online, some of which contains proper English. Download audio or video podcasts on your favorite subjects (tennis, anyone? how about ancient Egyptian poetry?) and pay attention to the language — what people are saying and how they're saying it. Your ear for good grammar will sharpen over time.

Listen to Authorities

Listen! Your teacher or boss probably says that word often, and you should (pause to arrange a dutiful expression) always do what your personal Authority Figure says. Apart from all the other reasons, you should listen in order to learn better grammar. By speaking properly, he or she is probably giving you English lessons along with descriptions of the Smoot-Whatever Tariff Act, the projected sales figures, and so forth.

Index

Symbols

A

H

hand-held devices, grammar rules for, 161–163

he or she, 43

he/his/him, 43

helping verbs, 16–17, 21, 25, 31

here, 29

he/she, 41

his/her, 41, 44

historical grammar, 6

homework, type of English used in, 150

homonyms, 151

however, 55

hyphenation, 96, 113–114, 142

hyphens (-), 113–114

I

I, 34

icons, explained, 2–3

if, 59

if/whether, 136

I/me, 146

in order that, 59

incomplete sentences, 9, 51

independent clauses, 56

indirect objects (IO), 48, 49

infinitives, 17–18, 63–64, 159

instant messages, 151

Internet, as tool for learning grammar, 167, 168

introductory words, punctuation of, 110

irregardless, as incorrect expression, 137–138

irregular plural possessives, 95

irregular plurals, 141–142

it, 34, 38

italics, 103

it/its, 36

its/it's, 37, 129–130

J

just, 83, 85

L

languages, capitalization of, 122

lay/lie, 134

less/least, 87

letters, type of English used in, 150–151

lie/lay, 134

linking verbs, 14–15, 17, 50, 76

little/less/least, 89

little/many/much, 89

lol (laughing out loud), 126, 161

M

magazines, as tool for learning grammar, 166

magazines and magazine articles, titles of, 103

main verbs, 14, 16, 21

manuals of style, 167

many/more/most, 89

masculine universal, 43

measurements, abbreviations for, 126

me/I, 146

memos, office, type of English used in, 150

MLA style, 167

more, 87

moreover, 55

more/than, 73

most, 28, 87

much/more/most, 89

N

names, capitalization of, 118

nearly, 83, 85

negative statements, 25–26

R

S

About the Author

Geraldine Woods began her education when teachers still supplied inkwells to their students. She credits her 35-year career as an English teacher to a set of ultrastrict nuns armed with thick grammar books. She lives in New York City, where with great difficulty she refrains from correcting signs containing messages such as "Bagel's for sale." She is the author of more than 40 books, including *English Grammar For Dummies, English Grammar Workbook For Dummies, Research Papers For Dummies, College Admission Essays For Dummies,* and *The SAT For Dummies.*

Publisher's Acknowledgments

Project Editor: Victoria M. Adang

Senior Acquisitions Editor:
Lindsay Sandman Lefevere

Copy Editor: Todd Lothery

Assistant Editor:
Erin Calligan Mooney

Senior Editorial Assistant:
David Lutton

Technical Editor: Faith Van Gilder

Editorial Manager: Michelle Hacker

Editorial Assistants: Rachelle Amick,
Jennette ElNaggar

Production Editor:
G. Vasanth Koilraj

Cover Image: © Kutlayev Dmitry/
Shutterstock